KIDADKILL

Spiderdadman
PUBLISHING

KIDADKILL

NO DEPTHS THE STATE WON'T STOOP TO

SPIDERMAN OF TOWER BRIDGE

DAVID CHICK

FULL ACCOUNT OF THE DAD UP IN LONDON

List of Illustrations

CONTENTS

Introduction

David Chick is a name most of you won't know nor will have heard of. But quite a few, particularly Londoners and those from West Sussex who are over the age of forty, will recall him from when he briefly relocated to Southwark on the 31st October 2003. He was the guy dressed as Spider-Man protesting on top of a crane by Tower Bridge for six days, over the state's abuse to him and his baby.

That protest was his fourth on the issue, and made news around the world when the authorities decided to gridlock a large area by closing Tower Bridge and nearby roads for the first five days he was there.

The issue of his story couldn't be more important. Central to it all is the 'family' law system, what goes on there, and the secrecy surrounding everything that they do. It's not possible for anyone to film the removal from your lives of your children in the 'behind closed doors' 'family' law court system, and so, people will never see what's really being done. Because of what 'family' law does, countless dads are taking their lives each year, as when their children who are their life, are suddenly stolen from them – often for no justifiable reason – it kills them. Just how many have perished over the years we'll never know, because, as with everything surrounding 'family' law, there are no statistics or figures on anything to be able to see just how serious this secret scandal is, or how many lives they've ruined and/or ended.

It wouldn't be a surprise if it were hundreds of deaths per year, they're responsible for. And with what was done to David and his daughter, he could easily have been one of them.

At the time of this protest, his little girl, Lauryn, was nearly three years old and the reason for David's protests, and she is his only child.

Like the majority of parents, he would do everything within his power to be with her, to love her, to care for her and protect her from any bad happenings, at least through to her adulthood.

No man in the world was happier or prouder than David when Lauryn was born on the 15th December 2000 at the Royal Surrey County Hospital, Guildford. But just ten months later, he and Lauryn were all but gone from each other's lives because that was how Jo, Lauryn's 'mother' wanted it to be. There were two options for David at this time, as there is for any dad faced with this most hellish of a situation: give up or fight. He chose to fight, there was no way that he would ever give up on his little princess.

Over the following months and years, he'd see just how the 'family' law system that's supposed to do everything in the child's best interests, would do the complete opposite. On realising this system had no intention of helping him, ten months after Jo had instigated her scheming and fabricated stories, in August 2002 he began protesting on top of construction cranes about what was being done and what was not being done in regards to the relationship between him and his daughter by these courts. He'd done nothing wrong and knew that none of what was happening to them, should have been. Their case could and should have easily been in and out of the 'family' law system within two or three months at the most, and with a completely different outcome. David had provided numerous examples of indisputable factual evidence to all involved in 'family' law by the middle of December 2001 – more than exposing exactly what was going on – if they wished to do anything in Lauryn's best interests. But because they didn't, their complete abuse and violating of David and Lauryn's lives, their rights to a private family life, and their basic human rights would continue for nearly five more years.

David had heard of numerous other dads' and children's lives being violated in a similar way by now, and his plan and aim was to do his utmost in exposing what was going on to as many as he possibly could. Over the following year, with the relationship between David and Lauryn having been virtually totally destroyed, his fourth lawful and peaceful protest made global news as he was dubbed 'Spider-Man of Tower Bridge' (and a lot of other things by the state-controlled media).

Ten months later and a year-and-a-half since he'd last touched, held, cuddled or kissed his daughter (in spite there having been a contact 'order' for them to see each other regularly throughout this time), his sixth protest was on top of the London Eye where he stayed for 18 hours. Each hour representing each month that there had been since he and Lauryn had last had any contact.

His story touches on many other issues related to how 'the Establishment' twists, covers up and uses harassment and intimidation to quell peaceful and lawful protests. In David's case, this has included abuse of power, malicious prosecutions, a litany of false allegations, arrests and charges, as well as psychological and physical intimidation and incarceration. He can substantiate virtually all of the claims in this story using a large body of evidence that he has meticulously compiled over recent decades which include: covert audio recordings of conversations and interviews, video recordings, photographs, e-mails, text messages, statements, police documents, printouts, letters and incident logs, 'family' law and criminal law documents, television news footage, and press coverage.

Some of you might think that spending over two weeks protesting, hundreds of feet in the air, on top of four cranes and the London Eye was somewhat extreme. Once you're aware of what it was all about, and what was done to David and Lauryn, I'm confident you'll see that his protests were no more extreme than what was done to them and their relationship, initially by the 'mother' and then by 'family' law. This is David's full story of all that happened, the lengths he went to in getting the relationship back for himself and Lauryn, and how what happened during those years damaged and affected the relationship between them.

Since November 2018, the authorities have begun a most blatant campaign of harassment and persecution against him all over again – which he has no doubt is because of his latest attempt to expose the secret, evil, state-sponsored kidnapping of, and abuse to our children by the 'family' law system. Coincidentally, this all commenced within a few weeks of his initial enquiries concerning writing this autobiography.

And this, after not a word from 'them' in over a decade.

Background

The youngest of three children, David was born in 1967 and lived most of his life in Burgess Hill, West Sussex, up until the age of thirty. His dad was a milkman and a part-time butcher, and his mum was a supervisor in Woolworths, later becoming a home help.

Playschool was fun, but after that it all became a bit too serious for David. It was the 'having to learn or you'll never get anywhere in life' philosophy that got to him, as that isn't always the case.

He enjoyed playing sports as a youngster; tennis, snooker and particularly football, but actual school work was never really his thing. He was the one messing about in lessons – the joker, the naughty one, a bit of a rebel – and was smoking and gambling before he became a teenager.

He left school with no qualifications, having no real ideas or plans for his immediate future, and his first full-time job was working at Tesco's. David had no responsibilities which suited him then, he was just living and taking day by day.

He'd supported Leeds United since he was about seven. He met his best mate John who was also a Leeds fan, down in the amusement arcades in Brighton around 1980. It was the mid-80's when David and John began following Leeds all over the country. Leeds was the most important thing in his life over many of the following years.

When David was 17, he received his first and only custodial sentence to date. That was when he was convicted of actual bodily harm after being involved in a fight in Brighton, for which he was sentenced to three months in a detention centre down in Aldington, Kent. He didn't enjoy that experience, nor the hurt it caused his parents in him being locked away. Being there for his 18th birthday wasn't great either, but it was all his own fault, and it served him right, and good.

After a few menial factory jobs that he hated, he found work that he enjoyed which was driving jobs. From then on, driving would virtually always be his way of earning a living. He loved the freedom of being out on the road, and of having no-one looking over his shoulder all day.

It was around 1991 that David first moved out of the family home.

He moved in with his girlfriend Tessie who had a little boy called Jason, who was about four. Tessie was top class although David didn't realise it at the time, Jason was one sweet kid and he enjoyed being his stepdad for the year or so they were all together.

David was close with his brother and sister at this time, and loved spending time with their young children – Hayley and Alex. David's always loved kids, playing with them and making them laugh; it's something that always felt and came so naturally to him, probably because deep down he was just a big kid at heart, and he couldn't or just didn't want to grow up. But he knows he's a decent person with a good heart though, which is why he resents the way in which his life and happiness has been ruined for so long, by a corrupt, faceless establishment, and numerous two-faced individuals.

In 1992, Leeds won what's now the Premier League, coincidentally this was when David had just started taking ecstasy, and so he was extra loving and extra happy about everything around this time.

Though not quite everything actually… as he was harassed, stopped, spoken to by the local Burgess Hill police on numerous occasions. Then they appeared behind him again with their lights flashing one particular night when he was just driving home and less than a minute away from his house. This would have been about the tenth time they'd hassled him in about a two-week period. David didn't stop, and just drove the last thirty seconds or so home, thinking to himself, 'Why won't they just fuck off and leave me alone?'

The police parking up right behind him outside his house with their lights flashing, resulted in his mum coming to the front door to see what was happening. Soon she was in tears seeing they were giving David – her baby, and her favourite – grief yet again.

The upset that this caused to his mum infuriated David, so the next morning he went to the police station and spray-painted 'ACAB' (All Coppers Are Bastards) and 'LUFC' on the outside wall, which probably wasn't one of his better ideas!

Within minutes he was arrested for his artwork, and later that day he was sectioned into the local psychiatric hospital. As soon as it was possible to do so David appealed his sectioning to a tribunal at the hospital, his appeal was successful and he was then free to go.

It was two years later, in the summer of 1994 that David had a fall-out with Simon Hancock, the landlord of The Junction pub in Burgess Hill.

David soon learnt that this low life was also the local (copper's nark) police informant. Hancock, accompanied by a couple of his bouncers, caught up with David a few days after their fall out and the nark whacked David with something solid during an altercation, splitting David's eyebrow open. Five minutes later, with David covered in blood and now in a sandwich shop that Tessie, his ex-girlfriend worked in, the police arrived and arrested David, soon to allege that he'd falsely imprisoned Tessie and the other woman working there, in the shop (this was solely done to get their nark off the hook for his assault on David). That quite serious (false imprisonment) charge could have seen David go down for years, and would have done if Tessie were prepared to lie like the other woman in the shop, who was a 'friend' of the nark, (but Tessie was only prepared to tell the truth in her statement).

The charge was serious enough to have David remanded

into prison, buying the police and their nark time to cover up the real and only crimes that day.

So, there was David in prison now, when there was no way he should have been.

For creating about the injustice of what was going on whilst he was there, he was soon given the mental cosh (injected with largactil) to shut him up, and before he knew it, he was back at the psychiatric hospital he'd been in two years previously.

The false imprisonment charge was eventually reduced to the much less serious charge of affray. The establishment could see how much they'd messed David up with what they'd done to him here. When 'his' solicitor told him, he wouldn't receive a custodial sentence if he pleaded guilty to affray (which it never was either), and that he would be released, David agreed to the 'deal' offer, as it meant it would all be over and done with, and his false imprisonment would be over.

By the time he was released, after having been incarcerated for months, David was at an all-time low. With all that had happened, his being falsely charged with an offence that he could have got years for, his being falsely imprisoned and being forced to take medication over the six months that it went on for, had all been a struggle for him to deal and cope with, as I'm sure this situation would have been for most.

Following this episode David was in a real bad way over the following months. For the first (and only) time in his life he was doubting his own sanity, thinking that maybe there was actually something wrong with him.

He hardly came out of his bedroom over the following weeks and months, he'd just lay on the bed, in a way hiding away, day after day; He wouldn't even wash himself (despite knowing he was stinking of body odour), wouldn't go outside the house, or even into the back garden – He didn't want anyone to see him in the messed-up state he'd been reduced to.

After months of being like that, his mum's love, support and encouragement somehow got him to pull through, and back on the road to recovery.

No-one else did, it was only his dear late mum and David at that time.

He'd improved considerably by the middle of 1995, but still wasn't great. In his down and depressed state, but wishing for some normality in the form of love and affection, David replied to a lonely heart ad in a local paper. The woman he replied to was a Lucy Garrett. She had a little boy called Aston who was also around 4 years old. Lucy soon told David that she worked as a special police constable which obviously didn't sit too well with him, but he carried on seeing her as he liked her, and Aston, and because Lucy seemed alright.

A couple of weeks after they'd met, Lucy told David that she'd been told it was either David or her job, and that it couldn't be the both, after obviously having been given an ultimatum by a work colleague or two!

Understandably she chose the job over David and that seemed the end of that.... Then a week or two later, she rang David and invited him to a house party (which seemed a bit strange after her reason for having to recently end all relationships with him) and then subsequently entrapped David into committing a petty crime whilst they were at the party. David has no doubt that Lucy was put up to the entrapment by one of her work colleagues, in order for them to be able to give him yet more grief.

David's head was far from great following the events of 1994 and early 1995, and now, here he was, in an on-off-on relationship with a police officer now suggesting that he commits a crime.

As freaky a situation as that was, David decided to go along with it in the hope that it might lead to him being able to prove or expose, and put a stop to what these local police bastards were doing to him.

Following his arrest, the search of David's house and him being charged, he was bailed with a condition – not to contact Lucy.

But as he had his own investigation to carry out, and evidence to obtain of how this crime came about and was initiated, that was a bail condition that would have to be broken!

On calling Lucy (the first of many recorded conversations David has, and which he did in order to prove the truth and the facts that would otherwise never be known) he got the evidence of exactly what could and should have put a stop to the police's abuse of power and crimes against him, only then for 'his' equally as corrupt solicitor to work for the other side and against David, in covering up what the indisputable evidence blatantly showed and exposed.

On top of Lucy admitting the crime was her idea during the conversation that David recorded, she also stated "the police all fucking hate you, and you best move right out the area because you'll never get a break around here," amongst various others during that call. Ian Elkins was David's solicitor on this case, and told David in the morning on the day of the trial to plead guilty but with mitigating circumstances. This was after his initial advice to plead not guilty, so that Lucy and the police would have to attend to be cross examined etc in regards to the 'crime', and in regards to what David's recording showed and exposed. But as soon as the judge heard David's guilty plea, he (conveniently!) chose to have no interest in hearing any of the mitigating circumstances, and so the police, the CPS, the Judge and David's solicitor between them (not sure if all of them were involved in it, though some definitely were) had managed to supress and cover everything up. The case was covered in David's local paper which mentioned "police conspiracy, and a disturbing tape", in the headline. And a quote by Elkins following the case, stated that 'the recording clearly showed that the crime idea was that of the policewoman'. But once again, the corrupt upholders of the law, and certain other 'professionals' involved in the case got away with their crimes whilst stitching David up once again, and just like that.

David was no angel in his (extended) youth and has 20-odd convictions between 1984 and 1999, with just the one that resulted in the (3-month) custodial sentence, mentioned earlier.

As this suggests, none were for anything that major or serious. David wasn't that bad and they were all for petty offences as he drifted through life without any responsibilities, much thought or any real direction. Some of them were also questionable (false) convictions, to say the least!

He got a 'lucky break' in 1996 when he met Laura who was from Burpham, Guildford. A few weeks into that relationship Laura invited David to move in with her which he gladly accepted. Not only did he like her very much, he also needed to get away from Sussex, as he knew even before Lucy had suggested it, and now thanks to Laura, he could. Being out of Sussex, it finally felt as if he could breathe. He soon found a driving job through an agency, and then found himself a permanent job. During the summer of 1997 David secured his first mortgage on his own first home, which was a studio flat in Leatherhead, Surrey.

In 1998 the relationship with Laura came to an end, and it was a couple of months after that, when David heard Jo, the woman who lived in the flat directly under his, sobbing one day. Being friendly and neighbourly… David went down to see what was wrong.

Jo told David that her dad, who had a bit of a drinking problem, had had a few too many whilst he'd taken her dog out with him that day, and had left him on a train bound for London. David gave her a hug to console her, the hug turned into a cuddle, which then turned into a kiss… and in no time David and Jo were in a relationship. Alan (the dog) was eventually returned unharmed, but David, Jo and Alan wouldn't all live happily ever after..!

It was in 1999 that David began working with and for Jo in the commercial cleaning business she had. Before they were aware of the pregnancy with Lauryn, they sometimes used recreational drugs together. For the millennium New Year's Eve, they'd booked a few days away in Dublin. Whilst driving through Wales to catch the ferry from Holyhead, they were stopped by the police who pulled them over for a spot check in the middle of the night. They had some cannabis and cocaine in the car for their personal use, which the police found. As any man would do, David said it was all his and that it had nothing to do with Jo. And that was another conviction for him.

A few months later in April 2000, David finding out he was going to become a dad made him decide that all his offending and drug using days were over with. During the years, from learning this through to Lauryn turning 18, David has just one conviction, which was for his fifth protest over the 'family' law scandal central to this story.

For the first time in his life, he had a reason to be responsible, and would now be 100% as responsible as any parent ever had been. His child would be his life; it was this that made him grow up and turned him into a man. Throughout the following years there's no-one who's faced up to the responsibility of having a child any more than David did. He's extremely proud of the person he became, and of everything he's done since.

The months that followed were happy ones. That year, David and Jo went on holiday to the Dominican Republic and Lake Garda in Italy. They worked hard and closely together in the cleaning business, selling both of their flats in order to be able to purchase a house in West Horsley, Surrey, which they moved into in August 2000. It was David's intention that this were to be the home that his baby would grow up in with two loving parents – it was his intention, anyway.

This most special period in David's life culminated when his beautiful daughter was born. That should have been just the beginning of a happy life for Lauryn, and of a loving relationship for her and David together with each other. But scandalously, father and daughter were set to be ripped apart, first by the 'mother' and then by the secret, sinister system that runs under the title of 'family' law - before Lauryn had even reached her first birthday.

1: There goes my baby

I was at the hospital for the birth of my little princess and it was the best feeling in the world when I watched her being delivered by Caesarean section at 11.56 am on 15th December 2000, weighing in at 7lb 14oz, on what was the happiest, proudest and most amazing day of my life.

Things couldn't have been any better... At last, my little family: me, Jo, Lauryn and Alan, the dog. A nice, two-bed house with a big garden in a lovely area, a thriving business and no money worries and, in fact, no worries anywhere. There'd been some struggles over the years in getting to this point but it had all been worth it as, finally, my life was exactly where I wanted it to be.

It was just a couple of weeks later when I first became aware of the fact that Jo was the one in charge and had the power and final say on things. I had assumed that Lauryn would have my surname, but when Jo and I talked about names prior to registering the birth, she soon made it clear that Lauryn would be having her surname and not mine. I wasn't best pleased about that, but it wasn't the end of the world and so I just accepted it.

I did get to choose the Christian name and chose Lauryn after the American singer, Lauryn Hill from the Fugees, rather than the usual version of Lauren. She had had various songs I really liked in the 90s.

Everything else was perfect, or so I thought, over the first couple of months following the birth, but in February Jo did something that shocked me and set the alarm bells ringing. She was sitting on the bed cuddling Lauryn affectionately like any normal loving mum whilst we were having a minor disagreement about something. Then all of a sudden, she threw Lauryn (only onto the bed, thank God) and stormed off downstairs. Lauryn immediately started crying as she landed on the bed. I picked her up, cuddled and comforted her and she soon stopped crying and seemed OK. Things were never the same between Jo and I after that.

To me, the only time you'd ever throw a two-month-old is if the house were on fire and you're throwing them out of a window to safety.

I mentioned this incident to the health visitor, thinking Jo may possibly be suffering from postnatal depression or something, as I was concerned about her and more so, about Lauryn.

The health visitor told me that she wouldn't be able to tell me anything she had discussed with Jo due to 'patient confidentiality' to which I thought, 'How wrong is that?'

Here was me worried about Jo and Lauryn and now I wasn't going to get any information back as to whether something's wrong with Jo. It was as though I'd just have to cross my fingers and hope that my little girl wasn't launched through the air again any time. Over the next few months, things gradually got worse between Jo and I.

It was as if she'd all but retired from doing any physical work and had become a full-time mum and I was just her full-time assistant, becoming more and more of a part-time dad in the process.

I'd often get in from doing our work and there'd be no sign of Jo and Lauryn for hours. If she wasn't at the gym having put Lauryn in the crèche there, they'd be at her parents'.

This to me, as well as other things she was doing, was Jo making things so uncomfortable and unhappy for me in the hope that I'd just go and walk out... but that was the last thing I was ever going to do by choice. That July we all went away on holiday together to Berrynarbor, Devon, for a week. Jo had booked this break a few months earlier. It was lovely being on holiday with my baby. This would be our first and last together, until over five years later. I've some photos taken from that one holiday of Lauryn and I on the beach and at the zoo and of Lauryn, Alan and I together.

Me and My baby, July 2001

Up in the air (like her Dad!) 2001

Jo didn't relent over the following months and in September she ramped it up another notch. During some little arguments we were having, she suddenly started calling the police.

She was now putting in a concerted effort in her attempt to build up a case against me.

Each time she called them, alleging abuse, violence or assaults by me, the police arrived, saw there was no evidence of anything that Jo was claiming – and left.

A police letter about one of them, stated that she called them on our landline at 6.10 am on the 3rd October 2001, asking for urgent police assistance. The police operator noted that Jo was heard saying, "Get away, you're scaring me!" and then the phone went down. Police units were dispatched to our address. The police arrived and Jo told officers that I was shouting and slamming doors. Officers noted that there was no violence and no injuries.

There was no violence and no injuries this time she called the police, or any other time she called them. Why was she 'asking for urgent police assistance' when no police assistance was required, let alone urgent!?

Who calls 999 asking for urgent police assistance because someone's shouting and slamming doors (not that I was even doing either)? And plus, the operator didn't hear any door slamming, me shouting or a word from me; they only heard Jo saying, "Get away, you're scaring me!" and, as for Jo putting the phone down as soon as she'd said that... really!

It was all about building up her 'case' against me... "*See, Judge, I called the police here, here and here because of this violent, abusive man who terrifies me...*" (even though I'd never actually done anything and she wasn't fearful of me in any way whatsoever) "*...so you have to protect me and our baby from him!*"

And now it was time for Jo to launch her whole scheming

plot, which would be backed 100% by the 'family' law system. She claimed anything and everything by me and against me, but there was no evidence of any wrongdoing by me. She'd claim she was terrified when the evidence proved the opposite. There was evidence of her threats and violence to me, but no evidence of any threats or violence by me. There was evidence of her throwing our baby. Later, there was her threat that she "really will play fucked up." And there were numerous other examples of her lies, fabrications and disturbing conduct and this was all within the first two months of her first solicitor's letter about the 'breakdown of our relationship' that she was claiming was as a result of my behaviour!

It was during the evening of Friday 19th October that Jo suggested we have a 'little break'. She put it to me as if one may do us good and potentially help our relationship. I wanted to save our relationship more than anything as I knew that if I didn't I would be seeing even less of Lauryn than I had been over the last months. And so I reluctantly agreed to her 'break' suggestion in the hope we could get back to how we were in the first couple of months after Lauryn's birth. Two days later on Sunday evening, I got some bits together, said my goodbyes and headed off down to my mum's house in Burgess Hill.

We'd agreed that I'd come back up the following Saturday to see Lauryn. It was on my arrival on that day, the 27th, that Jo gave me a letter from her solicitor that had arrived whilst I'd been away.

Her solicitor was Wendy MacLaurin of Hedleys, East Horsley in Surrey. The letter was dated the 19th, the same day that Jo had suggested the 'little break' to me..!

The letter began with, 'We have been consulted by Ms Joanna Gowens in respect of the breakdown of your relationship.' It went on to refer to my past history from nearly a decade previous… before going on to say, 'As you are probably aware, as an unmarried father, you have no legal rights in respect of Lauryn.'

So clearly, the break was never a break at all with Jo, having already instructed her solicitor we were over prior to her 'break' deception / suggestion to me. And as for the line about me having no legal rights in respect of my child, I took that as the threat that I am sure it was intended to be.

I wasn't aware at all, let alone having probably been aware, that I had no legal rights in respect of my child – how or why would I have been?

But I would have thought that my child would have had some legal rights in respect of her father, though!

The solicitor's letter was actually very tame compared to what Jo was about to claim had been going on over the previous six months. There'd be all the bog-standard and predictable allegations that certain 'mothers' come out with when they want rid of a partner/the father, with Jo claiming I was using drugs, was aggressive, abusive, violent and threatening to kill her and that she was the poor, 'terrified' female that wouldn't say boo to a goose. But there was not a shred of evidence to substantiate even one of her claims as they were all complete fabrications.

Now, I was totally aware of what she was attempting to do, so over the following days and weeks I gathered proof, exposing the fact that the only one of us who was making any threats or being violent was Jo and that she wasn't in fear of me at all, let alone terrified of me.

She'd now officially instigated her plan to have all that we had made and shared together, including Lauryn, all to herself… and there was nothing she wasn't prepared to do or say as she attempted to airbrush Lauryn and I from each other's lives.

I pleaded with her many times over the following days and weeks after receiving her solicitor's letter, to stop what she was doing. I even spoke with her mum, Margaret, and her brother, Marvyn, both of whom I'd always gotten on really well with, in an attempt to get them to reason with her.

Things were nigh on impossible by now in trying to reason with Jo but still I tried, as I couldn't bear the thought of not being there with and for Lauryn. After some persuasion, Jo agreed she'd come to Relate with me and so I booked an appointment for the evening of the 14th November. I'd booked it in my attempts for us to stay together, but I soon learnt that Jo was only coming for their assistance in us separating.

I arrived at our house in the afternoon of the 14th and Jo and Lauryn were out, so I thought I'd take the opportunity to have a look through her e-mails to see if I could unearth anything else underhand she may have been up to of late.

I saw that she'd been cautioned for a theft whilst she was pregnant with Lauryn, for obtaining property by deception. She'd kept that from me too!

And for a deception... 'How apt,' I thought!

If you put that caution alongside throwing our child at two months old, the drug conviction (that she only didn't have thanks to me) and her current attempts to deny her own child her father, whilst at the same time trashing everything about my life – this wasn't the nicest 'mother' in the village!

I printed out the last two years' business figures whilst I was at the computer that would later expose more of her conduct, which this evidence contradicted and also an e-mail conversation she'd had with a friend of hers, Melanie, which took place on the 29th October.

This was her conversation with Melanie:

Mel: Hi Jo, It was great to see you at the wedding, I hope you enjoyed it! and Dave.

Jo: Oh Hi there Mrs Turner hope you had a lovely honeymoon and wedding. Just a bit of gossip for now - me & Dave are having a break / split.

Mel: Oh how are you about you and Dave? sorry to hear… Is this still over the marriage thing?

Jo: No I don't love him anymore it has all gone! He wants to go to relate and has made an appointment for tomorrow. Dave agreed to move out on the basis that we are having a "break". Not sure about this though I just know I feel so much happier without him around. It is also to do with the gambling though, I found out that he actually hadn't given up, so a whole year of my life he has been lying about the fact that he is still gambling. Mel this is so crap I thought relationships were meant to be based on honesty. It's all a bit of a long story about how I found out so will save that until we meet. And anyway no trust, no love, & to be honest Mel I am not even sad. Just relieved that now I can meet someone nice.

By now, it was becoming more than obvious to me that there were no levels Jo wasn't prepared to stoop to and I knew I had to do anything and everything I could to gather as much evidence of the real truth, to show what was really going on.

I hoped to gain more evidence against her with the help of my Dictaphone friend during our journey to and from the Relate appointment.

This was some of our conversation during the Relate journey:

Me: Lauryn's just a weapon, that's all you use her for, yeah?

Jo: She's my little girl.

Me: She's my little girl, too.

Jo: Well, act grown up and you'll get to see her.

Me: I act grown up! OK then, OK. I've never fucking thrown her nowhere.

Jo: Yeah, but you're just moody.

Me: Yeah, but, yeah but… I took all the wrap for that coke shit and that was fucking both of us, yeah? You've done more drugs than me; so don't give me that bullshit.

Jo: I've got no drug convictions.

Me: Well, no, thanks to me, yeah. Do I get any fucking appreciation? No, do I fuck!

Jo: There's nothing on me, well, prove it with me.

Me: Prove what?

Jo: Prove that I've taken drugs; I could take a drug test tomorrow.

Me: You know and I know, Jo. You know and I know.

Jo: Even the solicitor said you'll still not be allowed to see Lauryn just for that, so if you want to start playing fucked up then I really will.

She'd carry out her 'really will play fucked up' threat most blatantly and with alarming regularity, over the following days, weeks, months, years and over the next decade-plus. Just as all of them in the 'family' law system would do too.

Jo knew that, because she had Lauryn, she had all the power and control and she was the only one making any threats.

Her telling me to act grown up and I'd get to see Lauryn when I was the only one who was acting grown up, leaving for the 'break' to try and save our relationship – that had no chance of happening as she'd already ended 'us' with her solicitor before she'd suggested it to me. I was the one acting as a responsible parent.

Her lies and threats weren't the actions of a grown-up person.

All I ever wanted was a relationship with my baby.

I hadn't played fucked up in any way, shape or form. It was her doing more than enough of that for the both of us.

And there was her "Yeah, but you're just moody" response when I mentioned about me having never thrown Lauryn. If she hadn't thrown her, she'd surely either deny it, say, "What the fuck are you talking about?" or something similar!

The following contains samples of some things Jo claimed were happening between March and October 2001 (the seven months prior to us separating) in her sworn statement to the family court:

David started smoking cannabis again and became aggressive and abusive towards me.

I became increasingly concerned about the safety of both Lauryn and myself.

I would frequently spend the evening at my parents' house because I was too scared to return home.

David took the phone off me and pushed me against a fitted cupboard, then tried to put his hands around my throat.

Another evening at this time David was behaving obnoxiously towards me. He threatened to kill me and yelled obscenities. I became extremely scared and, again, took Lauryn to my parents'. During the months of August and September, I stayed at my parents' many evenings and overnight on some occasions. If I needed to work, I would leave Lauryn with my mother rather than bring her back to the house.

David's behaviour was very erratic: he would easily become aggressive and often made obscene threats or threaten to do harm to me. These scenes were often in front of Lauryn. Whenever the situation became frightening I would leave, taking Lauryn to my parents' house.

David became more agitated and aggressive, he banged at the bathroom door while I was behind it and this broke the door. At this point I telephoned the police. David went to bed and ignored the police when they attempted to talk to him.

Her claims to the court were a cacophony of lies and there was never any evidence of one mark on her from my alleged assaults. I've never laid a violent finger on her (or any other female) in my life.

Would she really not have mentioned to Melanie any of the claims she was making to the court that she stated had been going on over the last seven months..?

All Melanie was aware of was a 'marriage thing' and the only and worst thing Jo was saying to her about me, in her 'just a bit of gossip' about any relationship problems, was that I gambled and had lied about it. Would Melanie really have been unaware of everything in Jo's version to the court – the aggression, violence, abuse and me threatening to kill her, as Jo claimed had been going on over the previous seven months?

As for her feeling so much happier without me around… I'll bet she did, with our child now all to herself, having gone from a tiny studio flat to a lovely two-bed house in a nice area, with the business having doubled whilst I'd worked with her and with twenty grand's worth of vehicles to show from the time we were together. And as for her line about 'honesty' – pass me a bucket!

It was also on record with Jo's doctor that she'd consulted them in August 2001 for advice on smoking cessation, when there was also a discussion of her general situation and it's recorded on the computer that her 'life situation's stable'. This was yet another contradiction to her version to the court, where she was making out her life had been the complete opposite of stable over the previous five months, since March.

And who was she more likely to be telling the true version to… a close friend and her doctor, or the system she was seeking assistance from in airbrushing the man who'd served his purpose and who she didn't want around any more, out of her and our child's lives?

Some of the other ridiculous and disturbing claims by her against me over the following months and years to the family court were: I sabotaged the loft ladder that nearly fell on her head; I'm a male prostitute and she wanted me regularly tested for AIDS; I delivered her some dog shit and a sliced open fox, with both supposedly resulting in the absolute worst-case scenarios possible involving Lauryn; I'm a cross-dresser; I'm a football hooligan; I'm a drug addict and that I threatened to slit her throat… to name just a few.

By now I was already heart-broken, desperate and in bits with what Jo was doing to Lauryn and I. I had no doubt that she'd been planning and plotting this for months and wasn't happy or impressed about the disgusting, underhand and deceitful way she was going about it. There wasn't anything clever or subtle in anything she was attempting; it was all being done in a completely selfish, despicable and blatant way.

After weighing everything up that had happened over the last month, it was becoming obvious that it was going to be impossible for me to stay with my baby.

I was in the house on the 16th November when Jo arrived alone, again, having left Lauryn at her mum's. We spoke for a minute or two before she suddenly flipped, began lashing out and trying to kick me. I retreated into the back garden to try and get away from her attack, before running past her, back into the house and locking the door behind me.

Then I saw her run towards the front door. As she attempted to get in, I got to the door just as she was coming in, and shut and locked it.

I'd had bucketfuls of psychological abuse from her over the months, but this was the first time she'd attempted to physically assault me. After gathering my thoughts for a few seconds, I opened the front door, ran past her as she attempted another kick and I was off.

As I jogged away from the house, Alan ran up the road with me, probably thinking it was all a game. Jo was following some way behind, screaming hysterically, "My dog! My dog!"

Not wishing for any harm to come to Alan as we were now on a main road, I held him for Jo to come and take him from me, but as she got to us her apparent concern for Alan disappeared as she went for me again. This was when I handed him to a guy who was doing something in the boot of his car on his driveway, who by now was watching on – for him to hand Alan to Jo.

This guy gave the following statement to my solicitor – what he witnessed that day. He said, "I saw a man in the middle of the road and a woman on the other side of the road shouting – she was clearly very agitated. I did not see the man act in an aggressive or violent way, or raise his voice at all. She was in a hysterical way, shouting as one would if chastising a child. She did say that she was alright."

However, the following is Jo's version to the court of what happened at the house that day:

I started to act aggressively, screaming at her and pushing her face when she tried to speak. I pushed her out of the living room. At this point she was terrified. I pushed her into the back garden and started kicking at her. I then pushed her out of the way and ran inside, locking the back door. She then ran to the front door and opened it with her key, as she tried to go in I slammed it against her head – this happened a couple of times. She used her mobile phone to call the police at this point.

Apart from her reversing around the truth of who was acting aggressively and doing the kicking, there was far more truth here than she normally quoted on 'incidents'!

Jo's statement that I ran inside, locking the back door and then she ran to the front door was actually true and a bit of a giveaway regarding who was attacking who...

Question: Why would I run into the house and lock the door behind me? Answer: To nullify being able to be attacked any more.

Why would she, if terrified and if having just been assaulted by me, want to get back into the house where I am, let alone be in a rush to do so? (She ran to the front door).

Why was it only when she was locked out of the house and unable to get to me, that she called the police? Any woman that was claiming what had just happened to her and who was genuinely terrified, would have used their mobile phone to call the police when I ran into the house and locked the back door (as we both stated I did).

She only bothered calling the police when she was unable to continue her assault on me, as she was locked out after I'd locked both doors to stop her attack.

The last thing any woman/person would do, having been assaulted by a man they're also claiming to be terrified of, would be to attempt to get into the house where 'her attacker/ the man' now was.

The police arrived and would have seen there wasn't a mark on her; otherwise they would have come after me for assaulting her, which they never did. So, what happened to her injuries from my kicks and the door head slams? Did they somehow vanish in those ten or so minutes? There wasn't a mark on her, or any injuries to her because she hadn't received one kick or any door slams to her head! And this wasn't her first fabricated door-slamming allegation, following her previous 999 call on the 3rd October!

On the 19th November, there was the first involvement from the court and, in a flash, power of arrest and non-molestation orders were put against me in the Guildford County Court, on the words alone of Jo's solicitor. There was no evidence of any violence or threats by me and there was already evidence of both by Jo to me, but the court was (somehow) satisfied that I had used or threatened violence against her and went on to say that there was a risk of significant harm to her if the orders weren't attached immediately.

Just what Jo's solicitor came out with I don't know, but I can imagine… and this was a hearing that took place with me having no knowledge of it. Then again, why would anyone tell me about it? I was just the dad/male parent.

And this from the 'family' law system that claims there's no bias, discrimination, or sexual inequality concerning the mum and the dad and that 'their paramount concern is for the best interests of the child/ren'!

With Lauryn being as good as kidnapped out of my life as she was now, it was the worst thing I've ever had to deal with. I was heart-broken, desperate, depressed and missing her like hell.

I wouldn't see her learn to walk, begin to talk, or hardly anything else over the following months (and years). My sudden removal and disappearance from her life was so wrong, unfair on her, no good for her, completely unnecessary and totally avoidable.

I could have given up and walked away, taken my life, turned to drink and/or drugs, turned violent or any combination of the aforementioned… or I could fight these two evils (Jo and 'family' law) to try to make things right.

I chose the latter, though I never imagined how difficult it was going to be. Every ounce of my energy, my whole aim and focus was to get my baby back and, more importantly – it was to get my baby her daddy back. The main thought going round in my head, apart from the searing hurt and pain and the odd suicidal thought, was the fact that Lauryn had done nothing wrong and she didn't deserve for her daddy, who loved her as much as any parent has ever loved their child, to not be there with her or for her.

There wasn't anything she could do about it, as she was only a baby when it all began.

I was fighting this on behalf of us both. I had to stay strong and do my utmost in putting right this most hideous wrong. Lauryn was my world; I would never give up on her and I would fight for her as much as any parent has ever fought for their child.

I got a solicitor as soon as those orders came through, Mark Barrell, from Mahany & Co in Horley, Surrey. He told me I was entitled to legal aid, but I told him I wished to get things going immediately and signed £10,000 over to him to get this sorted out ASAP, rather than waiting for legal aid to be granted, which would have caused delay.

I showed him the solicitor's letter, the e-mail conversation between Jo and Melanie, played him the conversation from the Relate journey and went through everything thoroughly that had happened so far. He was representing me in regards to three matters: Lauryn, the house and all my belongings at the house.

Straight away, I made him aware that all I cared about of the three of them was Lauryn and that we needed to be seeing each other as much and as often as possible. A couple of weeks later, Barrell told me a contact hearing had been scheduled at Guildford Court for the 17th January.

Jo's brother, Marvyn, was a good guy, and he'd agreed to host contact for Lauryn and I as Jo was making things all but impossible for us to see each other. Without Marvyn, we wouldn't have had any contact until after the court hearing in January at the earliest. He lived in a flat in Surbiton with his girlfriend, Sharon, who had a son called Jonathan aged about seven at the time.

Along came the next letter from Hedley's, which was dated the 5th December.

Barrell forwarded it onto me. Amongst other things it stated that Marvyn was only prepared to host one more contact (on the 15th December, Lauryn's first birthday) as my behaviour towards him and Jo's parents, had been less than acceptable.

I hadn't done one wrong thing to any of them; why on earth would I?

I'd never had a problem with any of them and the last person in the world I'd want to upset would be Marvyn; as I said, without him Lauryn and I wouldn't be seeing each other at all.

Also stapled with the letter was a £12,000 cheque from Jo 'for' me. 'Jo is concerned you should have money to live off,' her solicitor wrote.

Jo, concerned? No way, there must be a catch. The only one she cares about is herself – she doesn't give a shit about anyone else, even her own child, or she wouldn't have been doing any of this... And there it was, the date on the cheque was the 5th June.

So, Jo was so concerned that I should have money to live off since her bullshit had blown my whole world apart, that she'd sent me a cheque that could not be cashed, as it was now a few days after the six-month period that it had to be cashed within!

On Lauryn's first birthday, bubbling with excitement as I was to see my baby for the first time in over two weeks, I arrived at Marvyn and Sharon's, having brought my brother along with me to do some videoing, so I'd not only have Lauryn on video to be able to remember her first birthday and be able to see her whenever I wished, but also to hopefully gather some more evidence of Jo's lies, to go with the countless others I already had.

Lauryn's 1st birthday, as Marvyn looks on, December 2001

2: 'Family' Law and Mum Playing Really Fucked Up

Lauryn had just started walking by now, though she was still a little unsteady on her feet with the odd fall down. We hugged and kissed and cuddled and played and throughout our time together, on this day, all my stress of the last two months seemed a million miles away. The videoing was taking place as Lauryn, with a bit of help and encouragement, opened her presents. The bond of love between us was clear for anyone to see in the video.

Jo's mum, Margaret, was there who, according to Jo, was afraid of me and didn't wish to have any further contact with me. But she chatted with me in a relaxed and friendly way. She was clearly fine with me and did not appear to find me a threat at all.

With the video running to prove what was being said, I asked Marvyn about Jo's claim that this was the last contact he was prepared to host and the following conversation meant there was now evidence from both Jo's mum and brother, exposing more of her poisonous lies.

This was that conversation:

Me: Is it right, Marv, you don't want any more visits round here? I know it's not ideal, but apparently I've offended you, or something.

Marvyn: No, you ain't offended me, no; it's definitely not that, it's just the fact that it's not always convenient, do you know what I mean?

Me: Yeah, I understand that, yeah. I know it puts you out; basically, you'd rather be doing what you've got to do, like.

Marvyn: No, I mean, sometimes now it's cool because we wouldn't really be doing anything, but another time, what I'm saying is, it's not good enough for you just to see Lauryn when it suits us.

Me: Yeah, that's not right and it will be sorted out eventually.

Marvyn: It's not a problem to have it, but we can't do it as frequently.

Me: Yeah, yeah, I understand that. But what I got from Jo's solicitor is that I've offended you.

Marvyn: No, it wasn't like that.

Margaret (Jo's mum): No, no.

Me: Until proper contact's sorted out, Margaret, is it possible to see Lauryn at your house next time maybe, or not really?

Margaret: Well, I'm trying to sort that out.

Me: But I haven't offended you, have I?

Margaret: No. No, it's not me, it's John (Jo's dad).

Marvyn: I mean, it will be alright to do it round here.

Sharon: It's just finding... like Wednesday, it was cool last Wednesday, but it's (Sharon's son) Jonathan's school night.

Me: Yeah, right. I know it's not ideal and it's putting you out and all that.

Sharon: If it's not on a school night, I don't mind.

Marvyn: Thursday was cool.

Sharon: Thursday? But Jo said that's a bit inconvenient for her.

Marvyn: Yeah, but she can work something round that, though.

Sharon: Yeah, but Thursday was cool because we don't have Jonathan, it's not a school night.

Me: What, any sort of Thursday?

Sharon: I don't know, it depends. Any Thursday because Jonathan always goes to his nan's about half past four and his dad's most Thursdays and I don't have to worry about Jonathan getting to sleep or whatever.

Me: Right, right.

Sharon: You know, and I said to Marvyn Thursday was cool, I don't mind. But Jo said it was a bit inconvenient for her. I mean, I don't mind at all, Dave.

This case could and should have been over with any day now with the evidence there was and with the lack of evidence surrounding everything Jo was claiming.

And as for the evidence against me, the full extent of that were the words alone of Jo!

Can you imagine a more horrendous situation for any parent to be in than when your child's been as good as kidnapped out of your life, is being failed and abused by the law and it's the law who's also behind the kidnapping?

That was my situation.

It had been a couple of months so far and there would be over another four years-plus to go…

After viewing Lauryn's birthday video, my solicitor wrote to Jo's solicitor, 'The video does appear to contradict your client's comments regarding the conversation I had with Marvyn about Jo's claim that it was the last contact he was prepared to host.'

This was the standard of service I was getting from my solicitor…

It was actually another most blatant and vindictive downright lie from Jo to further damage and deny our relationship. The only grounds Barrell had to do as he should have been doing were moral ones, but as is so often the case, financial gain takes precedence over morals, nowhere more so than in the 'family' law system and especially when there's virtually no chance of getting found out – as no-one knows or hears about anything that goes on there. I'd all but done his job for him with the evidence I'd gathered and provided him with, but he didn't care about doing what he was being paid to do and ending all this in no time. He chose to do next to nothing and ate into the £10,000 that I'd signed over to him as much as he could.

His next letter to me said, 'I fully appreciate and understand as you have explained to me in our numerous telephone conversations, how aggrieved you feel about the way Ms Gowens is behaving in relation to all the issues. As previously stated, and I know counsel would agree with this, courts will usually favour a party who is seen to be acting reasonably. Dishonesty and unreasonable behaviour is usually frowned upon and viewed unfavourably by the courts.

'A court will undoubtedly have a great deal of sympathy with your predicament and I am convinced that Ms Gowens' bad behaviour to date will tell against her at the end of the day. I have deep sympathy with your predicament and will do all I possibly can to assist you. I can only reassure you again of my continued desire to act in your best interests and to bring matters to a favourable conclusion for you at the end of the day, but urge you to be patient and to bear with the courts who will deal with your claims in the right and proper manner as and when the time comes and give you a fair hearing, and I am sure, a fair outcome.'

Despite what he was saying and was aware of, he did nothing. I told him that Jo is mentally unstable and that I should be awarded residency of Lauryn. Her behaviour was clear to see to anyone and I instructed him to proceed with my residence application. (It was to be months later that I found out he never actually followed this instruction).

On the 17th January in Guildford County Court, a supervised contact 'order' was made for Lauryn and I to see each other for eight hours per month, split between Woking and Guildford contact centres… My solicitor told me that this was a step in the right direction.

In a very small way it was, as eight hours' contact per month is eight more hours than none.

But supervised contact for us was a completely sick joke of a decision...

...that was less than two hours per week at the most that I was now allowed to see my child, who had previously been allowed to be with her every hour of every day (when Jo wasn't out with her). So, from 168 hours per week, it was now to be just two hours per week at the most and it was to be supervised. And also, on top of that, Jo wouldn't even turn up for our two hours on four of the first times she'd been 'ordered' to and the court would do nothing to enforce their own 'order' that they had supposedly made in our child's best interests... what the fuck!

If either of Lauryn's parents' contact with her should be supervised, surely it should be the person where there's evidence they have done damage to her (and us) already – the one where there's evidence of having stated she was going to play 'really fucked up' regarding our relationship, who'd thrown her, who was emotionally abusing her in not letting Lauryn see her other parent and whose lies had resulted in me having to apply to the court to see my own child whom I should never have not been seeing in a normal environment, for one second. But that was it for me now – a maximum of eight hours' contact with Lauryn per month. As wrong as it all was, I could only accept it and make the best of my time with Lauryn at the centres. I took photos of her at virtually every one she'd come to and I have an album of our contact centre photos with the dates by the side. As sad as it all was, we still managed to have fun there, as I made that time together with Lauryn as good and as normal as I possibly could.

And in March there was to be a hearing to determine allegations of violence and drug abuse claimed against me by Jo – the many times over already proven that she is a violent, abusive, unhinged and compulsive liar. This was way beyond fucked up stuff that had already been going on for three months. All the evidence, for some reason, was being overlooked and ignored and the system was doing nothing in the child's best interests – as they're meant to do and claim that they do.

Later on that day that the contact order had been made, Jo would claim to the court that I phoned her, was threatening to kill her and that I was outside her/our house late that same night.

But not one call to the police by her this day or night exposed that for exactly what it was, which was proven within police correspondence detailing each call to them from her – with none made on this day!

A few days later Jo received some text messages regarding her offering sexual services that she attributed as being down to me. As with everything else she'd alleged against me, this had nothing to do with me either. The police looked into the messages she'd received and, although there appeared to be some evidence to back up what she was saying, for once, as in the fact that she was being contacted, there was no evidence of it having anything to do with me. This was also confirmed in the police printout on the matter, that stated, 'Unfortunately there was no link to Mr Chick.'

Them stating 'unfortunately' about there being no link to me – not only suggested they were hoping to find one and were disappointed not to have, but also that they'd investigated the matter vigorously in trying to find anything linking me to it!

This, by the police, was also consistent with what they said concerning the incident on the 16th November. This was the day where everything pointed towards Jo attacking *me*, but where they stated that I'd always be shown as the offender to the incident on that day!

It wasn't difficult to see whose side they were on, despite the evidence – and so much for them being impartial!

The 2nd February was the date of what should have been the second supervised contact.

I arrived early, in the hope of possibly getting an extra few minutes with Lauryn. I was standing at the entrance of the contact centre talking with one of the centre helpers, when Jo drove into the car park.

I was surprised and shocked, as well as gutted and angry when, 20 seconds later, she drove off with Lauryn still in the car with her. I was so desperately looking forward to seeing Lauryn for our two hours and, on realising I now wouldn't have the opportunity to see her, it all became too much for me. Not long after I broke down in tears.

Jo alleged that I'd threatened her at the contact centre when she never even got out of the car. The helper and witness from the contact centre who I was standing with when she was alleging I made the threat, confirmed that I did not threaten her, to my solicitor.

But the result of Jo's latest 'playing fucked up' stunt meant that there was no contact for me and Lauryn this day, or for the next three that had been 'ordered', with her claiming that she felt too intimidated to attend because of a threat that had never occurred!

The next letter from her solicitor said, 'This family has suffered from a degree of uncertainty and a sale of the property would be less beneficial to Lauryn than a period of stability.'

But two weeks later, Jo's apparent concerns regarding anything beneficial or otherwise regarding Lauryn evaporated, as the following letter stated, 'Our client is considering a sale as an alternative to a buy-out.'

Barrell wrote again, stating, 'I am sorry to say, as we predicted, she is using the allegation of your threat to stop contact. I have responded by seeking further details so that we can refer the matter to the judge and at least try and demonstrate she is not telling the truth.'

He'd already spoken with Stuart Alexander, the guy from the contact centre, who'd told him that I did not threaten her.

His 'at least try and demonstrate she is not telling the truth' line, when there'd been countless similar and worse untruths by her since day one and throughout, again showed he was doing the minimum , at most, on our behalf.

He also stated, 'I remain of the view that Ms Gowens has full intention of obstructing and interrupting contact on any excuse...' which was beyond obvious to someone with no intelligence. But he had £10,000 to do what was a simple, straightforward job because of all I'd provided him with and he'd had every opportunity to have nipped all this in the bud long before now had he done his job anywhere near properly.

I couldn't understand why everyone in this 'family' law system was playing in the exact same way that Jo threatened she would in the Relate journey conversation we had back in November.

The next time Jo allowed Lauryn and I any contact was the fifth one due, which was, by now, only two out of the five there should have been to date.

It was at the Guildford contact centre where the only one that had taken place so far had been over a month previously. I arrived early and was inside, waiting and hoping she'd show up. I was watching the entrance they came in through the previous time, when one of the helpers appeared next to me, holding a little girl. I looked at them very briefly before returning my fixated view back towards the reception entrance that I was expecting them to be entering.

I looked again at the little girl being held next to me and noticed she had her ears pierced, as Lauryn had too. And then I realised that the little girl I'd looked at plainly some ten seconds ago was my daughter.

I felt so bad for not recognising her straight away and for having looked at her plainly for those few seconds, as every time I'd seen her before I'd have given her a big smile, a cuddle and kisses straight away. I was overwhelmed with feelings of guilt, for the fact that Lauryn would have been thinking, for those ten seconds or so, 'Why did my daddy just look at me plainly and not smile, give me a big cuddle or any kisses, as he normally always does?'

She had changed a bit in the five weeks it had been since I'd last seen her; she had a lot more hair that was curlier now than before and as she was now a lot more mobile, toddling around for the last five weeks, she had lost some of her chubby, puppy face. I think these things, combined with the stress of all that was going on over the last few months, as well as the fact that I was totally expecting them to enter from the same door as the previous time, were what resulted in me not immediately realising it was my own daughter that day.

In March, I decided to visit a mutual friend spontaneously of Jo's and mine, called Sarah. Jo had known her about ten years and I'd known her for around three years. Luckily, Sarah was in and she told me Jo had recently rung her asking her to make a false allegation against me.

The following is a selection of Sarah's comments to me about Jo's call:

Like, at the end of the day, you know all it is you want to do is see Lauryn, isn't it?

I got off the phone and I was fuming, I thought 'That's bang out of order,' you know, and then, like, Andrew (Sarah's partner) spoke to her. I didn't speak to her at all then, I thought, 'Sod you!' because I don't appreciate that.

It's not right, I don't agree with it because I don't think it's right on Lauryn. It's not fair; who's going to suffer at the end of it all?

Well, I haven't spoken to her since because it just blew my mind, actually, that she put me in that situation. I thought, 'Fuck her, I can't be bothered.'

I said to Andrew, "I don't know how much more Dave will take of this, but I would have thought she'd have the brains to realise to stop, because he only wants to see Lauryn – he's not trying to do her any harm."

In March there was a psychiatric report made by the doctor who I was under following the events of 1994, to assist with what was going on in the family court case.

Dr Siddiqui's report and recommendations were:

'He is basically a quiet and shy person who functions reasonably well socially and has remained free from psychiatric symptoms since 1994, and has not received any formal treatment. Some of the recent events have affected his trust in other people. He is feeling stressed by his present social situation and is anxious about the outcome. In the last four years he has made a great deal of effort in rehabilitating himself socially and enjoying stability in his life, despite some lapses which he was able to overcome without any psychiatric help. He has expressed strong feelings of love and care for his daughter during interviews and stated that ever since the birth of his daughter he has played a major part in her care and upbringing. He has always taken interest previously in his brother and sister's young children in the past, and has enjoyed their absolute trust. In preparing this report, also my examination of him, did not indicate that he was suffering from any active or residual psychiatric symptoms. I am therefore in a position to recommend that he should be allowed to have regular and unfettered access to his daughter. On the basis of my assessment I have no reason to believe there is a likelihood of harm or neglect occurring to his daughter. He expressed considerable affection and concern for his daughter's future wellbeing and is keen to provide an active and caring role in her upbringing.'

Also around this time, Jo made her sworn statement to the family court for the hearing that was to determine allegations of violence and drug abuse by me.

Her whole statement was only consistent with all she'd been saying since she officially kicked all this off in October; full of fabrications, mis-information, lies, inconsistencies and contradictions that were plain for anyone to see, had anyone cared or been interested. I went through her statement thoroughly with my solicitor, pointing out and exposing, with hard evidence, proven lie after lie.

My solicitor told me he'd secured me the services of a 'very good barrister' for the impending hearing, Mr Dafydd Griffiths. I had asked him to provide me with a female barrister as I was thinking of every possible angle to assist and felt a woman representing me would have been more beneficial.

With no evidence to back or support even one of Jo's allegations, evidence to prove many of her claims were false and/or had never occurred and, with my 'really good barrister', I was thinking this surely would be the end of this nightmare. On my drive from Burgess Hill to Reading, where the hearing was being held, I was in a confident mood and looking forward to all Jo's lies and her conduct being exposed for exactly what it was, prior to getting the proper father-daughter relationship back for Lauryn and I.

But this day ended up being the day that resulted in over another four years' worth of abuse to us, thanks to 'family' law. It was Judge Critchlow who made findings of fact (based on the balance of probability) against me, despite evidence proving some of his findings were impossible to have been found. And as for the others he found 'against' me, there was nothing but Jo's inconsistent, contradictory and nonsensical words, as evidence on them.

The only explanation to his findings was because it's in a secret system and he's allowed to make any findings he so chooses to, despite however wrong they are, as no-one apart from me (the dad) would know or care, as no-one else would ever hear or find out about any of it... normally... or would they?

As with this system choosing to do and inflicting their evil on my baby and I, my response for what they'd done would be as far from normal as they could ever have imagined!

Critchlow found that I was violent, had been aggressive and threatening and had kicked Jo regarding the 16th November incident – when it was her attacking me, as all evidence, lack of evidence, plus her own completely nonsensical version of the incident in her statement about the day clearly showed!

He found against me, in that I'd made abusive calls to Jo and her parents, despite 9 of the 12 alleged calls, logged by Jo with dates and times having never occurred, as was proved by the itemised phone records I obtained and provided for my phone, where Jo had alleged the calls had come from. The other three calls, which had actually occurred, were calls to her parents that I made to see if they were able to assist with me seeing Lauryn at their house over Christmas. This was following the videoed conversation I had shared with Margaret, having said she would try and help out with this situation at Marvyn's on Lauryn's birthday.

So, despite 75% of the calls having never happened and there being nothing abusive about the other 25%, Critchlow found against me again!

He also found that I was responsible for the sex texts Jo received, the ones where the police had already thoroughly investigated and had stated, 'Unfortunately there was no link to Mr Chick.' So, now his 'balance of probability' farce 'findings' overruled and contradicted the outcome of the investigation by the police!

And he was satisfied – it was because I took drugs that our relationship deteriorated last autumn and, because of this, Jo went to live with her parents.

Jo had never even said she'd gone to live with her parents… just what fucking planet was this retard from?

And there were only the words of a proven compulsive liar saying that I was taking drugs last autumn (which I was not).

Just what fucking balance of probability is required on any or all of this parasite's findings?

And he finished off by stating that Jo had no objection to contact, that my relationship with Lauryn depended on me and that he hoped Jo didn't provoke and that I didn't invoke.

And do you know what? I hope for you, Critchlow… the longest, slowest and most painful one.

With blatant and categorical incorrect violence, harassment and drugs findings of fact against me, the hell years ahead were now set in stone.

So, I had Critchlow's farce findings against me that any proper legal system would have thrown out at the first stage as they were so flawed, beyond laughable and ridiculous.

And as for all the proven violence, threats, abuse and all the other shit Jo had been doing for the last five months, which there was indisputable and real evidence of and that would stand up and result in a conviction in a criminal court… The 'family' law system just ignored and overlooked the lot, as good as just sweeping them all under the carpet.

What my 'very good barrister' was doing this day I have no clue. I was sick and in total shock following Critchlow's so-called 'findings'. After the hearing, Griffiths told my solicitor that he feared I would dwell on the fact that findings were made against me, rather than concentrating on improving contact and addressing concerns raised.

Dwell on them..? No, not at all, Griffiths. It's fine having these damaging findings against me. Thank you so much for your outstanding efforts; here's your £1,500 for all your amazing work today. Could I give you a bonus for being so awesomely brilliant? Yeah, let's forget about the 'findings', they don't really matter at all. Join me for a drink, as I really need to celebrate this great result!

And as for me concentrating on improving contact, that's impossible for me to be able to do as the conversation with Marvyn on Lauryn's first birthday showed, as did the evidence of Jo alleging the threat outside the contact centre that never even occurred, to deny us contact on three of the first four that were due, etc. And as for addressing the concerns raised, *all* the concerns raised were flawed and wrong (as I can show and prove today) and so, how could anyone possibly address any of the raised concerns?

This abusing parasite really shouldn't be allowed to exist and neither should my solicitor who spouted similar shit following his conversation with Griffiths.

Barrell stated that the findings against me were by no means disastrous and, as the judge didn't disturb the existing contact order, effectively this was a result in my favour.

Violence, harassment and drugs findings against me couldn't have been any less disastrous – who does Barrell think he's (mis)representing… someone with an IQ of around three?

And as for his 'effectively, this was a result in your favour,' oh yeah, obviously… of course, it was… it's me who's got it all wrong and back to front!

Neither Barrell nor Griffiths made me aware that there was an appeal procedure in relation to that hearing and by the time I found out there was one it was past the date that the appeal needed to be lodged by. I dispensed with Barrell for doing Lauryn and I far more damage than good and for basically covering up and doing nothing with all the evidence I'd provided to him, as he pilfered over £6,000 from me.

I was now planning to represent myself.

Guildford contact centre, 2002

Woking contact centre, 2002

3: Time for a climb (or six)

Weeks and months went by… sometimes Jo turned up at the contact centre, but just as often as she didn't. I was going from Burgess Hill to Guildford or Woking each time, with the round trips averaging about two-and-a-half hours, whilst Jo's round trips, on the occasions she bothered, were under an hour. The times I'd get to the centres desperate to see Lauryn, after having not seen her for anything from a week to a month, depending when Jo last showed up with her, only to find her not having shown up again, you can't imagine what that's like unless you've had it happen to you.

Let me tell you, it was painful, heartbreaking and soul-destroying, not to mention the hour-plus drive back home, having not even had a glimpse of my child for another week and another week and then it was a month and then six weeks. Then I thought, 'Fuck this,' I've had more than enough of Jo and 'family' law abusing the relationship between Lauryn and I.

I'd done everything right whilst they had done everything wrong. I'd tried the system; the only system there is when our children are stolen from us.

Now I would find another way to somehow get my daughter back from them all.

I was not going to just do nothing and let them continue their abuse to my baby and I.

My aim became to expose how badly we've been treated and what they've no doubt done and are doing to thousands of other children and fathers throughout the country, in secret.

And then it came to me one day whilst I was driving in London. High in the sky and massively visible to many were loads of construction cranes dotted around… that was how my idea for protesting upon cranes materialised. I would come to make banners with messages on what I was protesting about.

This secret scandal needed exposing as much, if not more so, than any others and I felt that, being so visible hundreds of feet in the air would finally get me and this issue the notice it so desperately required.

It was August 2002 when I decided that London would be the best place to start my first climb (I didn't know at this point I'd need to do a second climb). I would ascend the highest crane I could find. I made a few banners – bed sheets spray-painted with my messages – packed my holdall with some food, water and other basics that would last me a few days and headed off to London to find 'my' crane. *(see opposite)*

It was Friday the 23rd August in Victoria when I began my first climb. It wasn't until I'd climbed up when it dawned on me that the biggest isn't always the best… well, not concerning what I was attempting, anyway.

But in the process I was learning how to make my next protest better, which would be pretty much impossible not to do after this one. I think the only person who knew anything about this first protest was the security guy on the site where the crane was!

Two weeks later I carried out my second protest. This one was in Guildford, within a stone's throw of the court where so much of the abuse had come from. It was also a lot closer to where Jo was living with my daughter, which was about six miles away. Whilst carrying out this protest I called Marvyn and said, "Things are looking up!"

Because the police had already contacted Jo at this stage about what I was doing, Marvyn already knew where I was. Then he said, "Why don't you jump?"

That was a bit of a shock to begin with; I wasn't expecting that from him, as he'd always previously been a decent human

1st Crane I protested on. Victoria, August 2002

being. But, at the end of the day, he's Jo's brother, and so him taking her side and now behaving like her too, wasn't a major surprise.

A guy claiming to be a police negotiator came up the crane and was trying to talk me down.

He told me that my family case would be looked into if I came down and that I wouldn't be arrested for trespassing on the building site where this crane was sited. Once I ended this protest, I soon learnt that everything he'd said to get me down had been bullshit.

It turned out he wasn't actually even police; he was a local press reporter posing as police. I was also arrested on suspicion of theft that Jo had apparently alleged whilst I was doing the protest (I have to make the point that we are not talking about stealing from the crane here). She claimed I'd previously stolen stuff that was actually my own property – *my* property that she'd refused to let me have over the last 11 months since she first conned me into leaving for the 'break'. The police eventually realised the belongings she had claimed I'd stolen were my own and, after having me in custody for hours over this, I was finally released without charge.

I had my first media coverage following this protest when a piece featuring my picture up the crane *(see opposite)* and the banners appeared in the *Surrey Advertiser* the following week with the headline 'Father takes his custody protest right to the top'.

This was a big leap forward from my first protest. I was being seen and heard now and people couldn't miss the issue that I was protesting about.

After having no control over anything in my life for so long, my protest was something I had total control over… which was a satisfying feeling.

And I couldn't ever really see the police or anyone attempting to come up to get me or force me down.

David Chick protests on the top of a tower crane in a custody battle for his daughter. (c)

Father takes his custody protest right to the top

A FATHER barricaded himself up a crane for almost two days in protest over a bitter custody dispute this week.

David Chick, 36, climbed up the crane situated at the development in Onslow Street, Guildford, at around 8.30pm on Saturday.

Police, fearing for may lungs, called in negotiators immediately but he eventually came down at his own accord on Monday at 10.30am.

He spoke with local several large banners to explain his protest was a desperate dispute over the custody of his daughter, and police say he was well prepared for the cold conditions.

When he finally came down Mr Chick, who now lives in Surrey

Hill after moving away from Guildford, was immediately arrested for a suspected theft which police said took place on Wednesday last week, September 4, and taken into custody.

While he was being interviewed he was also arrested for aggravated trespass.

Police said that as he refused to come down from the crane until Monday morning he delayed construction workers by several hours.

In a letter to the *Surrey Advertiser* Chick said he was driving up the crane because of discrimination against fathers in custody disputes.

Chick was later released on police bail until October 14.

2nd protest. Guildford, September 2002

I didn't know if my going public was going to make Jo or the system stop their shit at this time.

But if it didn't, my plan was to continue what I'd started and do it bigger, better and for much longer in the future and I wouldn't be stopping until I got my baby back and my baby got her daddy back.

Later this month, Jo sold our house with another swift kick in the 'you know wheres' for me.

She apparently sold it privately to the parents of a friend for £182,000, despite the fact there was also a £195,000 offer at the time through the estate agent from another interested buyer, a Mr Fisher. The £13,000 price reduction would have meant around a £5,000 loss to Jo also, if what she was claiming was true. But I don't think she knew what the meaning of the word 'true' was!

She may have been a lovely person... but generous was never her!

The highly likely scenario was that she sold it privately for around £190,000 and had pocketed the £8,000 difference, making herself an extra £8,000-odd, whilst at the same time robbing me of £4,000.

Towards the end of September, a letter from the police arrived concerning another fraudulent 'Jo act'. She'd invented a fictitious person, using the address of a friend of hers, as she attempted to screw me over for more money. There were two letters produced by the fictitious person/Jo, but the trouble I had on top of all else going on was that the police would do minimal – at most – on crimes committed against me, but the total opposite on any crimes alleged by me. Their letter said, 'The matter has been looked into, and with the limited investigation carried out it appears that Jo's letters dated the 2nd November 2001 and 10th May 2002 appear to be fictitious.'

You may have thought that if there appears to have been a crime after a limited investigation that they'd at least have a reason to investigate further, or perhaps even, God forbid, fully investigate...

...but, no. 'Unfortunately' on my behalf, it wasn't to be.

Not 'unfortunately' like they'd stated back in January when there was 'unfortunately' no link to me after their full investigation to try and find any sort of link to a crime being alleged against me!

Representing myself as I now was in our family case may have been OK but for the fact that Jo just ignored every effort I made to communicate. So, in November I was left with no choice but to employ another solicitor. They sent the standard letter to Jo that she'd been sent on numerous occasions already... 'Please will you comply with the contact order, you are clearly in breach of that order...' Blah-blah.

But Jo was more than aware by now that the contact order wasn't worth the paper it was written on. No-one cared or had done anything about her breaching and / or ignorance of it since the day it was made or throughout the last year. Because of this, in December there was to be a family court directions hearing that I'd requested.

Leading up to this hearing, she had only allowed us contact on two occasions out of the 21 we should have had since July. I had a barrister with me, provided by my new firm of solicitors and I was a little hopeful that that jerk of a Judge Critchlow would perhaps do something just and right in our case, for once.

What was I thinking of? As if this abuser was ever going to start doing anything right in our case. Perhaps I should be examined by a doctor for even thinking that!

He only went and reduced our contact order by 50% – from eight hours per month to four hours per month, stating that his rationale for doing this was that he hoped it would lead to consistent contact.

And do you know what I'm STILL hoping and praying for you, Critchlow..? The longest, slowest and most painful one ever for you.

What the fuck was that about? Am I missing something? How can this be happening? What is this system about? How can it be allowed to exist?

The point of my application for the hearing wasn't for him to reward the 'mother' and further abuse Lauryn and I – but that's what he did here and that was all he and the system ever did to us.

Time to sack another part of the 'family' law system after yet more 'family' law child abuse.

And another £2,000 wasted…

'Family' law bullshit claims that there is no bias towards the 'mother'!

There is no discrimination against the father!

Their paramount concern is for the child!

All they do is in the child's best interests!

Of course it is… how true and blatantly obvious – NOT!

Jo showing up at the contact centres was just as it always was – if and when she felt like it.

So much for Critchlow's brainwave about it leading to consistent contact, by cutting it in half!

On the 15th March, Jo, once again claiming Lauryn was unwell, cancelled another contact. I say 'once again' as this had been used too many times previously. She is generally a very healthy child. I was way beyond pissed off with Jo and everyone else in this whole system by now, as you can probably imagine. I knew there was no way Lauryn could have been ill on so many Saturdays over the last 14 months and so, early on the morning of the 15th, I drove up and parked near where they were living, which was now in Chessington.

Before long, Jo came out of the house with Lauryn, got into the work van and headed off. They were living about five minutes drive from where Jo's parents were living now and I had a fair idea that Jo would drop Lauryn there before heading off to do some work. As I followed at a discreet distance, I saw her van turn into her parents' road. They parked up and entered Jo's parents' house.

A few minutes later, Jo came out alone and drove off. So, Lauryn was apparently 'too ill' for contact with her dad but not 'too ill' for contact with her grandparents!

I made my way to the place I had a fair idea she would be heading and a little while later she arrived there, as I'd expected. My plan was to speak with her and try and reason with her. She disappeared into an industrial unit to do some cleaning and after a little while I went in to try and discuss things with her.

I had my recording device with me, not only to be able to remember anything that was said, but to prove my reasons for speaking with her if she claimed more bullshit, etc, by me. And you never know, I may have got evidence of more threats from her, or some other fucked up stuff.

But it was pointless trying to reason with her – there's no reasoning with someone who acts totally unreasonable, doesn't seem to know right from wrong and who knows no-one's going to do anything about them being that way anyway.

Jo had been ignoring my letters I'd been sending her, as at this time we were both representing ourselves and, speaking to her now, face to face, she was only trying to provoke me, wind me up and take the piss, as always. I was with her for about five minutes this day, asking her to stop all her bullshit and lies to the court and to allow Lauryn and I to have a proper relationship together, etc.

These few lines from our conversation that day show exactly what I was up against:

Me: Aren't you bothered about the damage you're doing to Lauryn?

Jo: Lauryn's fine.

Me: No, Lauryn isn't, she's missing her daddy like–

Jo: She's not.

Me: She's not? Lauryn's entitled to a relationship with me, yeah?

Jo: Yeah, and she's getting one.

Me: Two-and-a-half days in 17 months; you call that a 'relationship'? All this contact centre thing is crap, you know that.

Jo: It's all being sorted through the court.

Me: Sorted through the courts? Yeah, a waste of 20 grand. Wouldn't you rather spend it on our daughter than through the court?

Jo: Right, I would like you to leave.

Me: I thought we was having a serious conversation.

Jo: I don't want one.

Me: We've got a child that we should be talking about.

Jo: No, no–

Me: No, I haven't got a child any more, is that what you're saying?

Jo: I don't want to talk to you; go home and write a letter and I'll write you one back. I don't want to talk to you. (Oh great, so we were going to become fucking pen pals now!)

Me: I wrote you a letter last week, I've written you loads of letters and you say you haven't received them, re the psychologist months ago… haven't received it!

Jo: I didn't.

Me: Letter last week, you didn't receive that either, no?

Jo: Was it in a little envelope? (No, Jo, it was in a large, wooden crate!)

Me: Yes.

Jo: Oh, I gave it to Alan because he's sorting it. (Oh, please don't blame the poor dog now!)

Me: Who's Alan?

Jo: My boyfriend.

Me: Well, why do you give it to him to 'sort' for?

Jo: He just is in charge.

I finished off the conversation like this that day: "I've risen above all your shit, you provoke me as much as you like, yeah? You wipe my daughter from my life, abuse her and distress her and all that. I rise above you, yeah?"

And then I left.

The barbaric secret system and this sick woman were driving me insane. My solicitors had shafted Lauryn and I and, if I didn't have a solicitor, Jo just ignored all my correspondence.

The whole thing is just one totally impossible nightmare. Whichever way I go or turn, Lauryn and I were being failed and abused by them all.

Left with no option, I employed a third firm of 'family' law solicitors, Howlett Clarke Cushman, based in Brighton, Sussex. Third time lucky, maybe! As if... This one would do me as much damage as the first, if not more, which was something I wouldn't have thought was possible.

It was on the 28th March, after another month without any contact with Lauryn, when I drove to where her nursery was, just to get a glimpse of her. Jo's mum walked her to the nursery this day and saw me sitting in my car. Jo turned up about ten minutes later and soon there was a group of mums looking over towards me from outside the nursery entrance. A minute or two after Jo turned up, I saw her sitting in her van on her phone, probably calling the police again... and so I left and headed back to Burgess Hill.

A couple of weeks later I was arrested on Jo's allegations that I'd harassed her when I spoke to her on the 15th March and on the 28th when I went to the nursery, as she turned both incidents into nothing like what was the truth. She was just doing anything and everything to stop me seeing or from having any involvement with Lauryn, from harassing, stalking, etc, etc, because she could and because 'the system' allowed her to/ couldn't care less.

Then a few days later, she claimed that the police had

basically excused her from bringing Lauryn to contact any more, which was also complete bullshit.

Contact is a civil matter and nothing to do with the police. When I spoke with Kingston CID I was told, "I don't know who's supposed to have given (Jo) that advice (not to attend contact), but I wouldn't have thought that was advice that we would give."

She wasn't even bothering to come to contact any more anyway, so what was the point of her lie about the police excusing her from having to go to something that she already wasn't going to?

I also thanked Nicholas Soames, my local MP, for wasting more of my time and effort, whom I'd been to see previously about all that was being done to Lauryn and I. He had me provide him with various documents for him to forward onto the Lord Chancellor.

A lord chancellor, who was never able to do anything about what has happened in the court… What a helpful MP he was!

I had another solicitor, Paul Masters, representing me in the harassment matter. He was a criminal solicitor from the same firm, now representing me in the family case.

In May, he told me he was looking forward to receiving the recording of my conversation with Jo on the 15th March, in order for him to be able to listen to it. But the strange thing with this was, why would he even request it from me for him to then (mis) inform me that the recording was inadmissible and unable to be used in the forthcoming trial?!

His letter to me dated the 12th June, which I wouldn't have even received prior to the trial (on the 13th), stated:

'It will be a matter of attempting to character assassinate Ms Gowens, and counsel is fully aware of this. As I am sure you appreciate, this is a very dangerous thing to have to do, especially in front of magistrates, and the whole thing could go horribly wrong. Unfortunately, in magistrates' cases they are very much of the view that there is no smoke without fire, and question why the police would arrest someone unless there was a matter that should be considered by the court. Convictions are much more prolific in the magistrates' court than in the Crown court. Finally, you questioned again why audio tape of your conversation could not be used in this case, bearing in mind in other neighbour disputes videos, etc, have been admitted. The simple straightforward answer to this is that neighbour disputes are quasi-civil, whereas this is a criminal hearing, and the rules of evidence differ between the two sets of cases.'

Now I would have thought, actually, that it would have been of great benefit (and it would have saved me untold grief and a wrongful conviction) if Masters had represented me competently rather than negligently and not told me the recorded evidence was inadmissible when it was not (I hadn't just questioned him about it the once, either). It would have avoided the 'dangerous thing to have to do' that he mentioned and any possibility of it going 'horribly wrong', as well as showing how the police often arrest and charge men just on the words of a woman, when there's been no harassment whatsoever and any considerations about convictions in the magistrates' court being much more prolific – would also have been negated.

The 13th June was the day of this harassment trial. Without my (not) 'inadmissible' evidence, it was just Jo's word against mine. We were the only ones who knew I'd only spoken with her on the first occasion, trying to reason with her for the damage and abuse she was causing to Lauryn and that I'd gone near Lauryn's nursery to get a glimpse of her on the second occasion. But with no other evidence other than what Jo was claiming had happened in the two incidents, the magistrate came down on her side, finding me guilty. How they managed to find me guilty beyond any reasonable doubt when there was only her word against mine – and when I was innocent – was yet another example of the general institutional bias and discrimination against men and for women concerning false allegations.

After the trial I immediately informed my barrister, Louisa Cieciora, again that I was not guilty and that I wished to appeal the conviction. She strongly advised me not to, claiming, "In such a case as this, the chances of having the conviction overturned are slim and by going through the appeal process I would run the risk of a much higher sentence and higher costs."

I didn't care about her so-called 'advice' though… The judge got it wrong and so I would appeal and I didn't care about the risk of a much higher sentence or costs either. I'm not guilty of this offence and the conviction is wrong, just like virtually everything else going on over the last 18 months also was.

For weeks leading up to this trial I'd been preparing for my next protest. This one was going to be my best and biggest to date. I'd spent countless hours deciding on the wording for my banners before measuring, cutting and sticking the gaffer tape I'd use for the letters, onto the bed and dust sheets. There wouldn't just be two or three banners this time with scruffily spray-painted wording on – for this one I'd have a dozen. Some were dust sheets around 8 feet by 12 feet and the rest were single and double bed sheets. The gaffer-taped letters of my words were perfectly applied in black, making my messages easily readable and visible to all.

A photo of me taking a photo of Lauryn in her nursery playground, 2003

4: Spiderman of Tower Bridge

It was three days after the harassment conviction that I'd commence this protest and these were some of the messages of what my protest was about:

'UK COURTS DISCRIMINATE AGAINST FATHERS, ABUSE OUR CHILDREN AND VIOLATE THE HUMAN RIGHTS OF US BOTH'

'ASSIST OUR CHILDREN AND THE ABUSED PARENT, STOP ABUSING OUR CHILDREN AND ASSISTING THE ABUSING PARENT'

'FATHERS INVOLVED IN CONTACT DISPUTES WILL LOSE OUT VERY BADLY IN BOTH THEIR RELATIONSHIPS WITH THEIR CHILDREN AND FINANCIALLY'

'FAMILY COURT CONTACT ORDERS MEAN NOTHING. THE ONLY CONTACT WE GET IS WHAT THE 'MOTHER' ALLOWS US, NO MORE OR LESS'

'PARENTAL ALIENATION SYNDROME EXISTS, ADDRESS IT'

'OVER 50% OF SEPARATED 'MOTHERS' ADMIT TO THWARTING CONTACT (EMOTIONALLY ABUSING OUR CHILDREN)'

3rd protest. Tower Bridge, June 2003

I packed them into my holdall along with some food, water, cigarettes, my radio and other basics and headed up to London by train. The plan was to carry out this protest for a week or so. There were three cranes on the construction site by Tower Bridge where I'd decided to do this one. Climbing up to the top of the crane with my bag full of stuff was far more of a job than getting into the site and over to the crane, as security at the site was virtually non-existent.

It was at 2 am on the 15th June when I began my crane number three climb. Once I reached the driver's cabin, had got my breath back and had had a couple of cigarettes, I began tying all my banners along the jib of the crane. Then it was a case of waiting to see what would happen and just how many people I could make aware of what 'family' law was doing to so many. Within a few hours, police and other emergency vehicles started arriving down below on Tower Bridge.

It felt good as they got out their vehicles and looked up to me on my crane with all the banners, telling everyone about the scandal, failings and abuse by 'family' law. The secret wasn't such a secret any longer.

I felt empowered when I was protesting – it was like being untouchable. As I said, this was something, for once, that I was in complete control of. There had been nothing I'd had any control over for as long as I could remember before my protests and it was a nice feeling not being trodden over and taken the piss out of, as so many had done to Lauryn and I, for far too long.

A few hours later, police negotiators made contact with me and were trying to get me to come down. By around noon, there were about 20 F4J guys, including their founder, Matt O'Connor, milling about on Tower Bridge in support of my protest, waving their purple flags and drumming up support for the cause. This wasn't a major surprise; I hadn't hoped, suspected or even thought about whether they would support me as I was just doing what I was doing since the previous August. I could see numerous TV news crews filming down below and I was listening to the news that I was making on the little radio I brought with me, where the issue and my protest were being broadcast. I don't remember sleeping at all that night, but I do remember there being a lot of supporters down on Tower Bridge late into the night – which was great!

Before I knew it, it was daylight on day two, the 16th. By mid-morning, again, there were many down below in support of my protest and the police negotiators were speaking with me on a more regular basis in their attempts to get me to end my protest. But I was feeling good for once – after around 18 months of having felt the total opposite I was still planning to stay for the week, or so I'd planned.

The weather on both days was beautiful sunshine from dawn till dusk and there was one thing I was really enjoying, in amongst all the hurt and pain over my now two-and-a-half-year old little girl who I hadn't had any contact with for over three months at this point – this was the authorities all looking up to me and me looking down on all of them, which was just how it should have been with all that they had done, were doing and still would do.

It was during the evening of day two that I agreed to end this protest – it was, however, only after I'd been given certain promises by the police negotiators. But ending this protest when I did, rather than holding out for the week I'd planned, was one of my biggest regrets. I was told that what had gone on in my family case would all be fully investigated and that I wouldn't be arrested for trespassing on the construction site, or for anything else. The thought of my family case being looked into – finally – was the only reason I ended this protest so early.

I made a suggestion that Taylor Woodrow, the company whose site my protest was held on, could donate some money towards my cause as, after all, I was ending my protest a lot earlier than planned. And because of this they were able to re-start work on the site a lot sooner than they otherwise would have been able to, which resulted in them making money, days before they would have, had I not come down so early. I was told that they would consider making a donation.

But unfortunately, they decided not to donate any money to the cause in the end, which wasn't their greatest or wisest move (as they probably realised a few months down the line!)

Was anything done about what had gone on in our 'family' law case…

…as had been promised? No…

Was I impressed? No…

Would I return?… YES!

At the end of this protest a police spokesman said that they would not be taking the matter further. Police had no power of arrest as I was on private land. He continued, "We will send a detailed report to site owner, Taylor Woodrow, for civil redress if they wish." And a spokeswoman for Taylor Woodrow said, "We're not going to prosecute. Mr Chick came down of his own accord. We felt he worked well with the police and the protest ended peacefully. We are comfortable with the conclusion."

When I saw the piece that the Daily Mail had published on my protest, I felt good that I'd managed to tell so many about what was being done behind the closed doors of the 'family' law system but, at the same time, I was also gutted that I'd ended it so much earlier than intended. Contained within the article was a picture of my banners with my words concerning the failings of 'family' law, which were clearly readable in the picture the Daily Mail had printed.

This protest would have probably been the first time that the majority of the public would have heard anything about what really goes on in 'family' law and my thoughts were that, if I had stayed as long as I'd planned to, many more would have also been made aware – as there perhaps would have been more similar media coverage over the following days.

Now it was back to Sussex and the normal grind for me in my fight to get Lauryn back, dealing with corrupt solicitors and visits to the criminal courts that were mounting up, as well as to the family courts, when I should never have been having to attend any of them and wouldn't have been were it not for the goings-on by Jo, 'family' law and the police's despicable actions and conduct to me and my girl.

The next letter I received from Masters had been dictated on the 16th June (as that was what was written on it), but it was actually dated the 1st July. Why was there a two-week delay between it being dictated and sent? That was a strange one, or was it?

Masters began by stating that he regretted I was found guilty (of harassing Jo), which was weird to hear, as it was completely down to him and his negligent and corrupt representation that I had been found guilty.

Furthermore, there was mention of a report that would need to be prepared by the probation service (another waste of my time and effort, which was totally avoidable and unnecessary, like so much else). He stated that the magistrates had left all sentencing options open, which included a six-month custodial sentence (how nice – maybe he was trying to put me at ease and make me feel better!) and he enclosed my notice of appeal (against conviction) asking me to sign it ASAP, so that he'd be able to forward it to the court and the prosecution within the 21-day time limit, stating that the time limit was strict, that the notice of appeal must be received by both, no later than the 3rd July and that my 'immediate response would be appreciated'.

A few things jumped out at me here:

1) The two-week delay from the letter being dictated to it being sent out to me. Perhaps that was his attempt to make my appeal

out of time (and allow him to get away with his negligent and corrupt representation!)

2) His 'sign it ASAP' and requesting my immediate response when he'd not posted it out until two weeks after it was dictated – was odd!

3) And I got the appeal, despite it having been impossible for the appeal form to have been with them by the 3rd as it was already the 3rd when I received it – so both of them having to receive it by the 3rd was also more total bollocks from Masters!

Four days after I'd received that letter from Masters, I had to attend Kingston police station, where I'd be arrested on another false allegation of harassment by Jo.

After being held in the cells overnight and appearing before the court the following day (8th July), I was found not guilty of having harassed her this time!

This was the month I met Gemma. I was having a drink with a mate of mine, Pete, in a pub in Worthing, where Gemma was working behind the bar. I had an instant attraction to her and we'd be together for the best part of the next five years. I'll always be indebted to her for all the love, help and support she gave me over the following years. She was perfect in every way; I adored her and Lauryn did in no time too…

Throughout the five years of our family case, I 'won' or was found not guilty on over 80% of the criminal trials I was subjected to (six not guilty, one guilty). On average, over 80% of trials that go through the criminal court people are found guilty. So, my conviction rate through those years was the complete opposite, based on the percentages of the norm!

But then, in the family court, where the evidence is overlooked or irrelevant – that court as good as chose to find me guilty on virtually everything when I was guilty of nothing – which was as equally back to front as the criminal court figures.

Sentencing day for (supposedly) harassing Jo was the 29th July. I was sentenced to a curfew, to stay at my home address between 8 am and 1 pm Monday to Friday (that's me stopped from taking a glimpse of my child at nursery) for the next three months, plus I was to have a tag around my ankle to monitor that I was obeying the curfew. It also meant no more protests until the 30th October at the earliest, unless they were only between 2 pm and 7 am. As much as I had known that I shouldn't have been sentenced for anything as I hadn't harassed anyone, I had no real choice but to obey the sentence, as if I hadn't, the police would have come for me and I'd have been given further grief by them.

Shortly after this was when I learnt that the evidence Masters had told me was inadmissible was, in fact, not inadmissible at all and could and should have been used at the trial which, if it had been, I would never have been found guilty. He was already aware of the fact that my case was different to any others his firm had been involved in before, in the fact I'd already carried out two protests up cranes and, with him representing me after this, negligently as he had, there was no way I could allow myself to be misrepresented by that firm any longer – and so I sacked them on both the family and criminal cases.

I wondered why he said my recording couldn't be used, as that was surely something an experienced solicitor, as he was, would have known! It really beggars belief.

On the 31st July, Masters wrote, 'I trust that you are reasonably satisfied with the outcome of this case *(I'm absolutely over the moon about it, thanks for asking!)*, but I am aware that you intend to appeal against conviction *(intend to... I already had, through him and his firm, weeks ago!)*, however, it will be your intention to instruct other solicitors in respect of this particular issue *(correct, I can't be having you negligently/ corruptly misrepresenting me again!).*

May I take this opportunity of thanking you for instructing me in this matter and if I can be of any further assistance to you in the future please do not hesitate to contact me.' *(Further assistance… is this twat for real?)*

So here I was, without my daughter in my life in any way, shape or form throughout the last five months – a daughter and father who should never have been taken from each other for one second. None of what had been going on for the last 22 months ever needed to or should have happened (apart from, perhaps, for the first couple of months at the most). The 'family' law system had long joined in with Jo in the most serious emotional abuse of my daughter throughout this time. I'd now been wrongly found guilty of harassing Jo and was stuck indoors with a tag around my ankle due to 'my' own solicitor's negligence (and/or him being corrupt) on more of Jo's lies…

And the police weren't being particularly helpful to me either.

The joy of fatherhood, on separation, when the 'mother' is like that, when the laws corrupt and when the abusers are the law!

The only good thing about my curfew was that I now had loads of thinking time in making my next protest bigger and better than all the previous ones put together, but I wouldn't be able to do it until the end of October… I was not able to work throughout these years because my fight for Lauryn was far more important , and it was impossible for me to do both.

OK, the 31st October would be the date of the next protest – I hoped that 'family' law, authorities, the state and Taylor Woodrow would be ready for it!

In August I met up with Matt O'Connor at Charing Cross station; he'd been in touch with me a few times since my last protest. He'd already told me that his organisation's membership grew by a few hundred as a result of it, which was great to hear.

This day was when I mentioned to him my idea about dressing up as a superhero for my next protest, to add some humour into this most un-humorous of situations.

It appeared that he didn't think much of my idea at all at the time and dismissed it as not a very good one. However, just a month or so later he had two of his members do a protest dressed as Batman and Robin on a roof at the Royal Courts of Justice...

Him nicking my superhero idea and using it before I'd had a chance to wasn't something I was impressed about at all.

I was still naively thinking and hoping at that time that there must have been a firm of solicitors somewhere in the country who gave tuppence about the children and fathers stuck in that barbaric system....

And it was also in August that I employed my fourth firm of 'family' law solicitors, Margaret Walsh of Barnes & Partners, Edmonton in London.

She just sent yet another standard and pointless letter to Jo about her contact ignorance, stating, 'You have unilaterally ceased bringing Lauryn to the contact centre...' Blah-blah.

Clearly, the whole system was long broken and failing my child and I and now, nearly 20 years on, as far as I can tell, virtually nothing has changed!

I'd mentioned my next planned protest to a mate of mine called Ed (Eddie). He was a guy I'd met at an F4J meeting I'd attended earlier in the year. Ed asked me if I'd take one of their banners up with me on my next protest and, as we were fighting for the same cause, I agreed to. On the 30th October I drove to Dagenham where Ed lived. We'd already agreed that he'd take me down to Tower Bridge in the evening for my fourth protest to date (and second at Tower Bridge).

In the afternoon, Ed's mate, Mike, turned up with the

banner I was borrowing. It was certainly not little and must have weighed about 30 kilos. We left Dagenham in the early evening and headed down into Central London, parked up near Tower Bridge and then the three of us had a walk around the outside of the construction site as I worked out the best way in.

After deciding where I'd be getting in, we went to a pub and had a few drinks. At about ten o'clock we left the pub and went to see what the security was like on and around the site.

After my protest four months before on the same site I was expecting that they'd probably have upped the security since, but as far as I could tell it was no different to the last time.

Ed had also brought a pair of walkie-talkies so I'd have someone to communicate with and who could give feedback on what was happening from the ground, down in the 'real' world, as I wasn't going to be in the real world for the next week or so.

We returned to the car briefly, had a cigarette or three and a chat and then we got all my gear out of the car and headed back to the site. Ed had agreed to bring the large, borrowed banner over to the base of the crane for me, rather than me making two trips and because I couldn't carry everything in one trip due to the weight of it all.

Making our way from the perimeter of the site over to the crane wasn't that straightforward, with big holes and footings dug out everywhere and building materials to clamber over, whilst also trying to be as quiet as possible and watching out for any security staff. Once we'd got everything over to the base of the crane, Ed wished me luck and made his way back out the site.

Now, I just had to get everything up to the top and I'd be set.

It was at 1 am on Hallowe'en, the 31st October 2003, two days after the curfew that I shouldn't have been on, had ended, when I commenced this protest.

Getting everything up to the top of the crane was a job-

and-a-half. It was pouring down when I made that ascent which didn't help, plus I had a good 50 kilos to hoist 200-odd feet vertically up to the top of the crane.

My aim, as always, was to expose the sinister and secret 'family' law court system and to raise public awareness of exactly what they were really doing to countless children and fathers all over the country. This protest was on the same construction site as my third had been four months earlier in June.

I'd prepared my banners as perfectly as they could have been made, without having had them made professionally. The following were my messages written on my four banners I attached to the crane:

INSTITUTIONALISED SOCIAL SCANDAL.
ASSISTING 'MOTHERS' IN DESTROYING
OUR RELATIONSHIPS WITH OUR CHILDREN

ASSIST OUR CHILDREN AND THE ABUSED PARENT,
STOP ABUSING OUR CHILDREN
AND ASSISTING THE ABUSING PARENT

FATHERS INVOLVED IN CONTACT DISPUTES
WILL LOSE OUT VERY BADLY BOTH IN THEIR
RELATIONSHIP WITH THEIR CHILDREN AND FINANCIALLY

JOANNA GOWENS (THE SHE DEVIL),
CLEANING CO, CHESSINGTON, AND INCOMPETENT
JUDGE CRITCHLOW READING/GUILDFORD,
STOP ABUSING MY CHILD AND I

(and the one I borrowed was)
IN THE NAME OF THE FATHER

Checking what's going on down below! Tower Bridge, November 2003

It must have taken me a good hour, in two very stop-start trips, to get everything up to the top of the crane this night, for this job that couldn't fail and had to be done. It was just after 2 am that I was getting settled into the driver's cab and trying to get my breath back.

When I had, I tied the banners along the crane as the rain was still teeming down. Then it was back into the cabin to dry off and try to warm up… and then the next thing for me to do was to put on my outfit that I'd hired the previous week, from a fancy dress shop in Haywards Heath, Sussex.

I was becoming a hardened protester on top of cranes by now and, like most things, the more times you do something the better you get at it. I was determined to stay up this time for at least a week. With the tricks and lies done by the police on my last two protests I was more than wise enough to their games by now. I wasn't going to be talked down by a press reporter posing as the police like on my second protest in Guildford. And neither was I going to fall for any promises they might make (when they had no intention of keeping any of them), as I had done on my third protest. There was no way that I was going to let them get in my head this time.

A few hours into this protest at 6 am on day one, it was written in a police incident log that Detective Chief Superintendent Randall stated to Inspector John Stokoe:

1. The person on the crane 'knows what he is doing'
2. They are not in crisis
3. This is a political protest
4. Previous experiences of such protests shows that they can go on for days
5. The person is in total control of their actions
6. The person is not a direct threat to any other person or police officer.

Finally, he recommended establishing communication through local officers, adopting a low-key approach and:

'minimise attention he gets, no threat to self/others and will come down in own time'.

Everything that DCS Randall stated was true and correct, but what followed from the powers above were that they overruled everything he'd advised and ended up becoming the complete opposite of how he'd suggested my protest should be managed – kicked in.

When DCS Randall stated this, he was obviously unaware that a decision was to be made at a much higher level, about how the incident was going to be played out.

The police knew it was me (again), they knew it was my fourth protest on a crane, they knew I wasn't happy with their tricks and broken promises on my last two protests and they knew I was planning to stay up on this one for longer than any of my previous protests.

So, something serious and drastic had to be done by them to divert and deflect as many people's thoughts as possible away from the 'family' law issue that my protest was about, which the state wanted to keep secret… at any and at all cost… just as they would do for nearly a week.

At around 8 am this day, a decision was made somewhere by someone, firstly to close Tower Bridge and then to close the surrounding roads. The result was the main news coverage being all about the disruption, inconvenience and congestion being caused, rather than the issue my protest was about.

I couldn't believe what they were doing at first, but it soon dawned on me that by them turning the incident into what they had, it would not only divert most people's thoughts away from what I was protesting about, but would likely turn a lot of people against me and, ultimately, my cause. So, rather than it being a relatively small incident with virtually all news coverage and the public's thoughts being focused on the massively important secret 'family' law issue it was all about, it was turned into a much bigger incident but all to do with the grief being caused to thousands who were trying to go about their daily business, now stuck in hours of traffic jams.

It wasn't long before my first visitors arrived… a couple of guys from the police rope team who'd come to speak with me in an attempt to talk me down. One of them was Ian Spooner (Spoonsey, to his mates, who actually became a bit of a mate. Him also being a Leeds fan might have had something to do with it). They told me that I was causing all the road closures and grief down below. 'Pull the other one,' I thought. I knew there was no need for any roads to have been shut and told them exactly that. The only people who needed to have been inconvenienced because of my protest were obviously the crane driver and the site workers who needed material moved by the crane to be able to do their work properly. I found it intensely frustrating as it was never my intention to cause any disruption – I just wanted to expose to the public what is being done, in secrecy, to our children and us. I didn't want to be everyone's bad man in stopping them going about their day. I was just portrayed as the annoying guy dressed as Spider-Man pulling a stunt and stopping all the traffic, by the 'unfree' press manipulating the truth at the request and on the orders of the state.

But the games had begun, we were only a few hours in – and the level of it had gone up drastically compared to my June protest. Now, it wasn't only Jo and 'family' law playing the really fucked up game as she had threatened on the Relate journey – now the police and authorities were playing the same way too.

Them making it into a major disruption and inconvenience issue to so many and trying to make me believe it was all my fault, wasn't happening. I'd decided long before now that I wasn't going to let them get in my head with any of their games, lies or bullshit this time, however hard they tried.

It was as if they were treating it like a game of dare or chicken and I had no intention of bottling it, giving in, breaking, or backing down before they would. Spoonsey and his buddy, McAllister I think his name was, came back up a couple more times that day, repeating the same crap from their boss that they'd told me the first time we'd met.

During the evening it was quite nice up there, all alone in the dark. It was so peacefully tranquil and whichever way I looked I'd see fireworks exploding..

I had a panoramic view for miles in every direction. I think I got an hour or two's sleep this particular night in the driver's seat of the cab, but I don't really recall. What I do recall is that it wasn't that warm, but then again, it wasn't exactly the warmest time of the year and, of course, the further you are from the ground the less warmth there is.

Day two was Saturday and I remember it was blowing a gale.

There were many families visiting the Tower of London, which was on the opposite side of Tower Bridge from where I was. Quite a few times I heard young kids shouting out, "Spider-Man!" that were walking round the Tower. I looked over and saw many kids (and some of the adults) waving. When I waved back I heard the kids cheering excitedly because they'd got Spider-Man's attention – that made me feel good and it was a nice feeling hearing happy, cheering and excited kids. As they returned the waves it made me think of Lauryn, not that she was ever much out of my thoughts. 'What I'd give just to be able to wave to her right now,' went through my mind several times. It had now been seven months at this stage since we'd last had any contact – seven months since I'd touched, held, cuddled or kissed her and, having not been able to do any of those things for so long was hurting beyond words.

But I knew I had to put all my emotional and physical strength together, push those depressed thoughts out of my head as much as I possibly could in order to stay strong. I had a most important job to do and there was no room for weakness or me failing to see this through for the week, or so I'd planned. That was not an option.

In thinking about Lauryn during my protests, I wondered how she was, how much she'd grown and changed since I'd last seen her and when I was likely to spend time with her again. I never doubted we would be back together one day, but I had no idea when it would be. I didn't know if it would be in a few weeks, months or years...

Each time the police rope team guys popped up for a chat with me to try and put me on a guilt trip over the disruption down below in an attempt to get me down, it was always on "health and safety grounds, we can't open the roads whilst you're still up here." Blah-blah.

'If you say so... fine, whatever,' I thought to myself, already beyond bored of their predictable bullshit! What else was being done? The 'family' law system had never said that I couldn't see, or have access to Lauryn.

I think it was in the evening on this day that I received a phone call from a guy who said he worked for the *Evening Standard*. After a few words, he asked me if it was true that I had a drug conviction. Being honest and not lying, unlike so many I was up against, I answered him truthfully and told him that I did have (it was the one I'd taken all the wrap for on Jo's behalf, on the way to Ireland).

That was all the skank was after, and once he had his little gutter press piece he was gone.

I spoke with Ed on the walkie-talkie, mentioned what had just happened and we had a laugh about how sad the guy and the press are.

I did a few more trips from one end of the crane to the other and a climb to the highest point to stretch my legs, break my boredom and to try and warm myself up a bit. I then took in all the free firework displays going off everywhere, whilst thinking of my girl.

Sunday arrived and nothing had changed down below. By now, I was getting pretty pissed off with the road closures as, no doubt, tens of thousands of others were too. I asked Spoonsey why the roads all remained closed when he next came up. Again, he said his governor was saying that there was no way the roads could be reopened until my protest had ended. Talk about blackmail! The crane was nowhere near any of the roads and I knew they were talking bollocks.

Before I knew it, it was Monday – day four. I was staying strong, holding firm and had no intention of cracking or caving in under the pressure of what the police were telling me with what they were doing or with what was being said in the news reports, which I had been listening to on my radio. I spoke with Ed a few times most days and he relayed back to me words of encouragement and that actually a lot of good stuff was being said and written, despite what the authorities had scandalously turned my protest into.

Listening to the Nick Ferrari show on LBC helped me somewhat though, despite the negativity of much that was being said and done against me by the police and the authorities through the media. I heard various listeners that had phoned in to Nick's show, who were supporting what I was doing, as well as backing up what I knew to be true about the whole handling of the incident by those in charge, in that there was no justifiable reason for any of the roads to be shut.

There was still no sign at this point that the authorities were about to end the gridlock situation they'd created all around Tower Bridge. I had a bird's eye view of the traffic jams and hardly anything was moving down below, whichever way I looked.

Cars, lorries, taxis and buses were stationary and bumper-to-bumper everywhere and with Tower Bridge being completely clear and empty of any vehicles, except for numerous emergency vehicles, it made everything even more weird and surreal.

4th protest. Tower Bridge, October & November 2003

5: The suicide plot

Soon there were certain defamatory and derogatory remarks being added into the news reports I was hearing. One was from a 'top' police officer and another from Ken Livingstone, the Mayor of London at the time, the same Ken Livingstone who supported the IRA back in the 80s when they were blowing up Londoners.

Dick (Richard) Barnes (Deputy Head of the Metropolitan Police Authority) spouted, "It's not an option to tell a police officer to climb up that crane and drag that prat down. What Spider-Man Flybrain's doing is beyond the pale..."

And after Livingstone had been briefed about what to say, he said, "Every other idiot with a grudge will think they can just get up and inconvenience a couple of million Londoners and get away with it. Mr Chick was amply demonstrating why some men should not have access to their own children. The idea that an individual can hold London to ransom is completely unacceptable; we would not put up with it if it were Osama bin Laden. I do not see why anyone would expect we would put up with it for this man. He is putting his own life at risk, as well as the lives of police officers and Londoners. He is also causing huge inconvenience."

The following are a selection of the media's headlines and comments during this protest:

He's campaigning for rights, better rights for fathers.

Police say they are trying to get the man down, but until they do that they cannot open Tower Bridge.

One man has gone to unusual lengths to draw attention to his plight regarding being refused access to his daughter, closing down part of Central London in the process.

Trained negotiators have been brought in to try and talk the man down; until they manage this, the bridge will remain closed and there will be severe delays.

His aim was to help estranged dads to get better access to their children; he hasn't achieved that goal as yet but he has managed to bring part of London to a near standstill. Tower Bridge remains closed until he comes down and nearby roads have been cordoned off.

A father dressed as Spider-Man snared commuters in 25 miles of traffic jams across Central London yesterday... (and mention of fathers' rights).

Spidey's protest fiasco – he's cost firms up to £50 million in lost trade... (and mention of access rights).

It is totally unacceptable that this man's foolish protest is causing massive disruption to London and holding Londoners to ransom. He is bringing misery to thousands and costing businesses money. It cannot be allowed to continue.

The near gridlock he continues to bring to much of the city... (and mention of fathers' rights).

Ludicrous, how Spider-Man protester fighting for access rights to his daughter has brought chaos to London traffic... (and mention of access rights).

Masked maverick faces arrest after sparking traffic chaos with Tower Bridge demonstration.

Crane protest costs £5m a day as father holds city to ransom... (and mention of fathers' rights).

Paralysed by Spider-Man.

Caused traffic mayhem in London... (and mention of access rights).

Spider-Man's 40-mile jam. Traffic jams totalling 40 miles condemned parts of London to gridlock until last night as the 'Spider-Man' protest went on. 'Whatever sympathy people might initially have felt for this man has evaporated.'

Police have brought in trained negotiators to bring the man down; until they manage this Tower Bridge will remain closed.

How can one man single-handedly bring London to a standstill? That's the question the Met police are facing tonight as David Chick, aka Spider-Man, prepares to spend his fourth night up a crane by Tower Bridge. He's protesting the plight of fathers who are denied access to their children.

Do you have any sympathy for the man who's brought London to a standstill? Has he strengthened his case for fathers or just made the public completely lose patience?

Police are under attack, not only from the motorists fed up with the disruption, but also from the protestor who's been throwing what's been described as human waste at the police.

Chick has caused chaos for commuters and held Londoners to ransom.

According to local residents, this is no friendly neighbourhood Spider-Man.

He's been criticised for chaos costing millions of pounds. He hasn't got the right to totally disrupt London. He's deeply angered local people.

Sadly, rightly or wrongly, sympathy does seem to be turning against him.

He's not only putting his own life at risk, he's risking the lives of police officers below.

Not one mention anywhere amongst them about 'family' law – the issue of the protest!

Only some mention about contact and fathers' rights, but nothing about the children's rights!

And 90% are not particularly favourable words regarding what I was doing!

The following quotes are taken from angry drivers stuck in the traffic jams, which they believed were down to me (duped by what was no doubt being pumped out by the authorities through the media):

"He's doing something very stupid."

"He definitely won't see his daughter now."

"He should be brought down one way or another; this is ridiculous, it's taken hours and hours to do an hour's job."

"Get him down; drag him out."

"It's absolutely ridiculous; get him down, get him off."

"It's taken me an hour-and-a-half to do a quarter-of-an-hour('s) journey."

('An-hour-and-a-half'? What about how long it's taking me to get the 'family' law system to stop their abuse ?)

So much for democracy, human rights, freedom of speech and a right to protest, etc, when all is covered up and twisted into whatever 'they' wish to portray to everyone through the state-controlled media. As for free press… all's corrupt, just like so much else.

The media were plainly singing from the same hymn sheet, which was undoubtedly drawn up by the authorities and with strict guidelines that they had to adhere to:

1) Do not mention anything about 'family' law.

2) Blame Mr Chick for all that was being done to the tens of thousands caught up in the congestion and gridlock around Tower Bridge.

It was no coincidence that the two words, 'family' law, were not once mentioned anywhere by any genre of media throughout this protest, when that was clearly and solely what all of my protests were about.

And only one banner ('In the name of the father') out of the five that I'd tied to the crane, was ever shown in any of the media coverage; again, to keep the real issue of the protest completely secret. There were, however, various mentions of my protest being about a father's access rights to his child and about contact, but there was never anything mentioned about the child/ren's rights. Nor was there ever any mention of the emotional abuse being inflicted on them or our basic human rights being violated by the 'behind closed doors', 'family' law system responsible for it all.

There were just a few choice words from Jo during this protest, which were, "Have I fallen off yet?"

(She's lovely really!) And if she were to say what she thought about what I was doing, it would all be swear words.

It was around 6 pm on day five (4th November) when I first mentioned to Ed that I was going to end my protest the next day. Within an hour of me informing him of this, everything down below changed… The cordons of the previous five days' blocking off of the roads were being dismantled and Tower Bridge itself was being opened up, as were the other roads. What power!

Of course, they had to try to turn this around to their advantage. The latest game/tactic, when giving it a little thought and that you didn't really need to have been Einstein to work out, was…

'The protest, which had been going on for five days (and which could have been going on for many more days) ended within 24 hours of us reopening the roads… wasn't that (reopening the roads) a great move by us… as it got him to end his protest… how clever was that by us!'

This was also one of the routes they'd try using in their attempt to have me prosecuted on the public nuisance charge. But, unless the health and safety laws were changed around 7 pm that evening, which seemed pretty unlikely, it wasn't exactly their cleverest move.

As with them reopening the roads, they'd gone against and exposed all their previous bullshit, where they'd been stating for the first five days, 'We can't open any of the cordons or roads until he is down and his protest has finished.'

I could imagine them all by now – gold–silver–bronze (Pinky and Perky) and other high-ranking police officers and members of the Establishment all sat in a room somewhere thinking,

'Mmm, we need to do something serious here now as we've just made ourselves look like complete bullshitting twats by doing the complete opposite of what we've been saying throughout the first five days,' i.e.:

Police say they are trying to get the man down, but until they do that they cannot open Tower Bridge.

Trained negotiators have been brought in to try and talk the man down; until they manage this the bridge will remain closed.

And the conversations, wherever they were going on, were no doubt to work out their next move and they could have been something like this:

"We need to ideally remove or at least minimise any chance of Chick/Spider-Man from being able to show us for what we are and for all that we've done... does anyone have any ideas?"

And after a period of silence, some (sick) someone comes out with, "How about trying to shame him into jumping, using that conviction he has from the 80s?"

"Well, if no-one else can think of anything else... (silence) OK, let's give it a try," (as they descend deeper into the sewer that they have permanent access to).

And so someone with access to the Police National Computer (PNC) passed that story to Mike Sullivan, the crime editor of The Sun, for it to be in the next day's edition, no doubt with a little backhander for the 'favour'.

They could have gone for a story about my 'numerous convictions', me 'being violent', my 'drug use' or about my 'previous medical history'... but no, they went for the one conviction that was nothing like any of the others, to make me look like a dirty perv – a queer – as that was the story most likely to shame me into jumping, as I have no doubt their team, thinking about my mental state at the time, would have worked out!

The next day their whole page story appeared with the headline 'Spider-Man's a pervert'.

'The Sun' joins in on the suicide plot, November 2003

This was what that story related to…

I was in Lancing, Sussex one night when some guy told me there was a girl parked up in this car park giving away free 'head'. I went over to the car that I could just about make out, as the car park was unlit and it was dark. Within a few seconds of my 'freebie' commencing, two plainclothes police with a torch suddenly appeared and we were caught in the act. Both of us were arrested as to my shock, horror, and disgust, the 'girl' in the car - wasn't a girl. This 'incident' resulted in me receiving a 'gross indecency' conviction (for my being duped/stupid/careless at worst, and whatever way you look at it, this doesn't make me as quoted in The scum Sun's headline!).

I had received various convictions before I had the responsibility of knowing I was going to be a dad as I've already mentioned, from assault occasioning actual bodily harm (ABH), handling counterfeit money, criminal damage, possession of drugs, drink-driving and I was a bit of a mad Leeds fan to most who knew me.

Now, the bastards were purposely trashing my entire image; they were using a historical conviction, which was questionable to say the least, and which was obtained by police entrapment. I've since learnt that it was a widespread tactic they used at the time I received it.

I'm pretty sure I've read that, because so many of these convictions came about from entrapment, they're automatically removed from your record if you do what's needed to have them removed.

As for Mike Sullivan who ran the story, he actually apologised to me for having done it when I contacted him about it, asking who gave him the info. He'd later be arrested over corruption allegations involving illegal police officer payments. How apt!

Press, police – all of them with any power are as corrupt as they come.

I was just one desperate dad up against all these highly

intelligent police officers and authorities, using whatever array of devious, disgusting and corrupt tactics and strategies they decided to use in their attempts to discredit and destroy me and all that I was lawfully and peacefully doing. They were in control of everything that was being done surrounding my protest, as well as everything being said and written about it. The only thing they weren't in control of was the actual duration of it.

It was stated through the media (via the police), and you probably noticed the statement earlier, that I was throwing human excrement at the police. Later, the police admitted I never had.

No way would I have ever done that – my shit's far too good for them!

By this stage, many were beginning to see through the police lies, the twisting and the cover-up and, towards the end of my protest these were some headlines/quotes:

'Spider-Man a nuisance? No, he's a national hero.'

"Very powerful and humanitarian cause, all power to him."

"After losing contact with my daughter, I really, really know where he's coming from. I really sympathise with him. I know how desperate you have to be to do something like this. Fathers love their children just as much as mothers."

"Hats off to the man, it's the only way. Parents and kids are suffering, but no-one's listening."

'Superhero to the dads denied kids.'

"Extraordinary attempts of a desperate man."

And day six, Guy Fawkes Day, the 5th November and the last day of this protest had arrived… 'What a mad five days, so far,' I was thinking. Though personally, they weren't that different to my previous 700 or so. It was nearly as consistent in a scandalous way as to how Lauryn and I had been ripped from each other's lives.

On this day I turned on my radio and, after being the first and main news story mentioned for the last few days, it wasn't like that any more. There was just a brief mention at the end that Spider-Man was due down today and that he would be arrested for causing a public nuisance.

Me, a public nuisance? Fuck off; a public and humanitarian service is what I'm doing.

It was a well-known fact that I was coming down that afternoon and that I planned to end my protest at the time 15.12, which is Lauryn's birthday. I had told Ed and the police that this was the time I'd be heading down.

Around 2 pm the police rope team guys suddenly turned up nearby with a coffee and a packet of cigarettes for me and asked if I was still keeping to my word about coming down this afternoon, which I confirmed I would be doing. They said Ed had been trying to speak to me on the walkie-talkie and I told them my batteries had died – not that it mattered now though as I had no need to speak with him any more as I was virtually on my way down.

When they left, I thought how out of character that was, them bringing me coffee and cigarettes. They hadn't helped me once in any way whatsoever all week, and had done their utmost to damage and twist everything my protest was about. Apparently, they did it as a goodwill gesture I'd later read in one of their incident logs. Goodwill to me from the police? Pull the other one!

And now, the very, very lowest and sickest of blows from those in control would come to me.

Just before 3 pm the police returned to visit me again, but this time it was to provide me with replacement batteries for the walkie-talkie. Even more strange I thought, they'd been giving me all sorts of crap and bullshit all week and hadn't done me one favour... but in the last hour they'd brought me up a coffee and some cigarettes... and now another trip up to give me some batteries (so I was now able to communicate with Ed, who I'd no reason to speak to at this stage!)

I hadn't asked for them and didn't need them though... what was really going on here and why were they, at this very late stage, suddenly 'helping' me with anything?

Then they informed me that Ed needed to speak with me, so I put the batteries in the walkie-talkie. It was now around ten minutes prior to me starting my descent down, prior to my being arrested and taken off to wherever it was I was to be taken.

On speaking with Ed, straight away he told me about the piece in The Sun.

I didn't think that my heart could've sunk any more before he relayed that to me, but when he told me – it did. Anger was my first emotion, but soon it turned to feeling gutted and then panic, with all different thoughts flying around my head. Then it was disgust that there were no sick depths these bastards weren't prepared to stoop to in their attempts to break me. A brief thought about jumping to my death and ending everything came over me, before I took a deep breath, pulled myself back together and thought, 'Fuck you, disgusting, despicable, corrupt, low-life, child abusing bullies – you've failed yet again in your latest sick attempt to destroy me.'

And no, I won't be jumping or falling anywhere, for you... I have a daughter I love and want to see and who deserves to have her daddy in her life – not for him to be dead before she was 3 years old because of your sick and sinister cover-up games.

I could imagine the headlines if I'd jumped... ['Spider-Man – a nuisance no more!']

The cover-up machine would have gotten away with all their evil bullshit and hardly anybody would have batted an eyelid or be bothered to seek out the truth of what had really occurred. Any questions about the handling of the protest would have evaporated (not that hardly any were even raised, despite the week of contradictions and bullshit, the grief caused to hundreds of thousands trying to go about their daily routine and then the complete opposite being done in opening everywhere up before I was even down, as they said would not be possible all week), not to mention the pending prosecution for being a public nuisance, which they had, at best, only a slim chance of succeeding on – that would have all conveniently disappeared too.

The 'goodwill gesture' visit, of providing me with coffee and cigarettes prior to the second visit with the batteries, was their attempt to make what they were hoping for seem less blatantly obvious had I done as they were hoping – and jumped.

So, that was their nasty little surprise to be played out to me before I reached the ground (however I'd arrive there!) There was my interview to look forward to (if I made it), plus the court hearing. But would I be bailed or held on remand (where something similarly sinister could easily have been organised for me)?

When I next spoke with Ed, he told me that the police had given him a copy of The Sun that day and said that there was a bit about me that he should tell me all about, otherwise he'd also get arrested on the same public nuisance charge as me, for conspiring in it.

He relayed it to me rather than him also being arrested on that false charge, which I understood and had no problem with him having done.

I'd had the crushing pain over what had been done to Lauryn and I by the system for the last two years, I wasn't particularly looking forward to meeting the various police personnel shortly, being in a cell or being interviewed on the false charge they were attempting to have me convicted of.

Being aware of what they'd turned my latest peaceful, lawful protest from and to, in order for the secret to remain secret, had pissed me off. I was wary of anything else they may have been planning, up their sleeve or otherwise. I was hungry, tired, fatigued and dirty and had been coping with all the psychological warfare that had been waged against me over the last six days by them and so I wasn't in the greatest place I could have been as my protest was just about to end... Now, I was hearing that the whole country was being told that I was a pervert (on top of all the other lies and unpleasantness that had been stated by those in control during the last week). The 'team' against me would have been considering the state of my mind throughout the duration of the protest and it would have been highly likely they'd have been in regular discussions with some sort of expert psychiatrist person in regards to what would have been going around in my head that week, plus what the state of my mind was likely to be. It's a shame they didn't spend one minute doing anything right or decent surrounding the protest.

And I'd also put good money down that they thought and hoped that, with me hearing about their story that it may very well just push me over the edge – literally.

The only things I was controlling were the duration of the protests and myself. Their attempts to influence how it would end were no different to how Lauryn and I were being treated by 'family' law.

Had I done as they'd hoped there would have been a few more lies and another little cover-up by them and in no time all would've been forgotten as they often do, however corrupt and blatant their actions are. Just think of Hillsborough as an example, where it was eventually found that the police and authorities were accountable for the deaths of 96 Liverpool fans that occurred, with millions watching on live TV. They initially got away with their mass cover-up, doctoring countless statements, etc, in hiding the criminal evidence of what really happened – before, they had blamed it all and much more (with the assistance of the same scummy newspaper they teamed up with against me) on the Liverpool fans, causing even more untold grief and heartache for decades, to the families and friends of those they murdered there.

They'd already covered up the main issue of my protest all week. Would they hesitate in another cover-up here against just one man, if I had jumped?

As I've numerous examples and proof of and know only too well, there's no level they're not prepared to stoop to in twisting and covering up the truth to save their own skins.

There's obviously no way that I could prove me jumping was their hope or plan, or would possibly be able to prove it, but on the balance of probability (a phrase I picked up from my – just as fucked up – family court case) with the varying degrees of, albeit, only circumstantial evidence, it's at least likely through to considerably likely that this was what was being desired by whoever organised it all; from the leaking of the story that evening in time for it to be in the paper the next day, for it to be able to be relayed to me whilst still up on the crane (after they had heard me say I was ending the protest the next day), to providing me with batteries and through to them persuading Ed to tell me about it.

But just like all the other games they attempted against me that week, again, they failed miserably. Not only Jo and 'family' law playing 'really fucked up', but police, authorities and the state also!

And as for my actual descent? As a result of that conversation with Ed, it occurred an hour or so later than I'd originally planned, after I'd digested what he told me.

There was quite a crowd gathered down on Tower Bridge, with various news and camera crews. It was about four o'clock when I started that delayed descent. I could hear quite a few cheers as I was climbing down.

A few minutes later I reached the ground where I was greeted by about five police officers and I was officially arrested. As they escorted me out of the site there was a lot of clapping and cheering coming from a group of 50 or so, who'd been waiting for me to come down. I put my hand up to them, still with my full Spider-Man suit on, including my hood, before being placed in my awaiting carriage and being swiftly driven away by the upholders of the law – to the police station for my interview.

6: Nine months without a glimpse of my girl

Sir John Stevens, the top UK police commissioner and, at the time head of the Metropolitan Police Service, stated the following garbage, cover-up and lies on BBC London News, the day I ended my protest:

"I'm perfectly happy with the operation initially, but once I decided that conditions had changed we reopened; we have to take note of health and safety considerations for the public and the police and it was a successful operation overall. But we will review it, we are very concerned about congestion for Londoners; we don't want people stuck in traffic jams and anything we can do to minimise that in the future we will do."

In response to Stevens' tripe statement, the weather conditions he referred to changed from very windy to dead still on day three and the reopening of roads didn't occur until the evening of day five!

As for his 'successful' operation line, this can only relate to the fact that they were successful in nothing having been mentioned anywhere or by anyone in regards to the issue the protest was over – 'family' law.

Was it successful in angering, inconveniencing and disrupting hundreds of thousands of members of the public's lives who were stuck in traffic jams for hours on end over five days, because of all the congestion his team purposely caused? Surely not!

Were the tens of millions of pounds of costs to the economy and local businesses, which were being quoted, a success? I wouldn't have said so! And as for his last line on his concerns about congestion for Londoners – as mentioned above – that was exactly what had purposely been done to hundreds of thousands over the first five days, because of their chosen tactics!

Years later, in regards to 'Operation Midland', Stevens (a hugely respected figure at the Met!) stated, "What needs to happen is for the full truth to come out. It's as simple as that. The best thing in these situations is to have full exposure and transparency, especially with something which has caused enormous damage to the victims and also to the reputation of the police service." Talk about pot and kettle; maybe he should try putting into practice as he preached on this... Full truth... transparency... enormous damage being caused to children and dads... reputation of the police service!

They could have easily (and legally) prosecuted me for contempt of court, slander or defamation for naming Critchlow on one of my banners and for stating that he was a child abuser. Predictably though, I wasn't prosecuted over any of those. If I had been it would have taken place in a criminal (non-secret) court where reporting was allowed, which would have given rise to an opportunity for media coverage and the possibility of some exposure about the 'family' law system that the authorities don't want anyone to hear about, consider, think or know about. And so, there was obviously to be no charge or prosecution on any of those; in fact, there was never any mention (or a photo) of that banner anywhere during the protest. I did eventually find just the one, which I came across on the Internet months later.

There was never any mention either in any newspapers or TV news reports, it was as if it was never there – vanished or had been airbrushed from existence. The only banner shown on TV or in the press was the 'In the name of the father' one that I'd borrowed, again, suggesting that my protest was all and only about – dads' or fathers' rights issues – which it certainly wasn't only about at all once anyone saw past the twisting and cover-up of what it was all turned into.

My interview at the police station lasted for an hour and

throughout it they were trying to trip me up into admitting that I was a public nuisance for what they'd done. They also suggested that I'd only ended my protest because they'd reopened the roads (when the truth was, as I have explained, they only reopened the whole area once they heard me mention I was planning to end my protest the next day, and virtually as soon as they heard me say it). Talk about turning it on its head... Playing stupid games with me still... bored!

The following are some pieces from my interview (that should never have even been taking place as it was the authorities who purposely caused the nuisance to the public, not me) for you to get a gist of the game with DI Roberts:

DI: What do you understand by being detained at the police station on suspicion of having committed the offence of causing a public nuisance; what do you understand by that?

Me: That I've been a nuisance to the public, apparently.

DI: OK, I put it to you, Mr Chick, that you have come down today because the roads were opened; that's right, isn't it?

Me: No.

DI: But you've decided to come down early and I put it to you, that the reason why you've come down early is because last night the roads and the cordons were reopened allowing traffic to flow freely. That's right, isn't it?

Me: Well, no.

DI: OK, so when you were climbing up the crane–

Me: The second one or the first?

DI: On the second occasion...

Me: Right.

DI: Yeah.

Me: Yeah.

DI: ...what did you think was going to happen?

Me: I thought I was going to do my protest.

DI: Yes and, as a result of that, what did you think was going to happen, as a result of your protest?

Me: There'd be some publicity.

DI: Right, so what consequences were you hoping for as a result of your protest?

Me: To make the public aware of what's going on with fathers and children in the family courts.

DI: And how were you going to do that?

Me: By doing a protest with my banners up.

DI: I see. Why were you going to do your protest on a crane as opposed to, for example, in the street, with your banners?

Me: Bored.

DI: Forgive me, Mr Chick.

Me: No.

DI: But I came down to your protest site yesterday…

Me: Right.

DI: …and you'll have to excuse me, but I couldn't read the signs on your banners from the crane, some of them.

Me: Right.

DI: Right.

Me: Erm, em…

DI: So, I tend to have fairly good eyesight, I tend to have good eyesight.

Me: Right, so have I.

I presume the DI wasn't doing too good as DS Rogers then took over:

DS: One of them (banner), I think, has been a little bit derogatory about your ex-wife. Is that right? Your ex-girlfriend.

Me: A little bit derogatory?

DS: Yeah.

Me: It couldn't be derogatory enough.

Or was the DI getting ready for his finale, as he came back and finished off with:

DI: OK, finally David, I put it to you, that you went up onto that crane the second time, having experienced the consequences of a protest you carried out a few months before, that you weren't satisfied with the consequences of the first protest, because it didn't cause enough chaos and thereby give you more publicity.

So you went up on the second occasion, I put to you, intending to gain maximum publicity, knowing that the only way you were going to get publicity is causing disruption to the people in the locality, lawfully trying to go about their business. That's right, isn't it?

Me: No.

DI: And by doing that, I put to you, by doing that you went up there intending to cause a nuisance to the public. That's right, isn't it?

Me: No.

END of interview.

If only they could have somehow managed to get me to believe them and got me to admit that I'd caused what they'd caused, then I would have had to plead guilty to the public nuisance charge, and their bullshit and chosen tactics of inconveniencing so many people's lives in order to cover up the secret scandal, would have been a total success.

Later that evening I was charged with the offence of 'public nuisance' and was to appear at the Thames Magistrates' Court the next day, following my night in one of their five-star cells! Compared to my previous week's sleeping quarters, not that I got round to doing much sleeping, it actually was a bit like five-star accommodation, but just one night was enough, thanks!

At the hearing, the prosecution seemed hellbent on me being held on remand and so didn't want me to get bail for some reason. But they lost and failed again as my defence team did the business and secured my being bailed, albeit with various conditions and following lots of legal arguments. I had to stay at my address in Burgess Hill every night, or at Gemma's house in Worthing. I was not to climb any tall structures, whether buildings or otherwise and I couldn't display myself in a fashion which was likely to cause disruption or inconvenience. But it's fine for them to do both!

Getting bail was a huge relief. If I had been remanded, my being silenced could easily have been arranged in more ways than one. The fact that they'd put up such a fight in their attempts to have me remanded, suggested to me that something just as sinister (as The Sun story and battery episode of the previous day) could have been being planned.

Some people don't make it out of prison alive. It could easily have been arranged for someone to permanently silence me and the authorities would have preferred me not being able to say anything concerning the 'events' of the previous week and, even more so, anything else about 'family' law!

This would be the first of three malicious prosecutions that I was subjected to within 11 months of each other between November 2003 and September 2004. This was because I'd become a thorn in the side of the authorities in my mission to expose 'family' law with my high profile protests.

There are four elements of the tort of malicious prosecution, which are:

1) I must have been charged: I was charged with the offence of causing a public nuisance.

2) The charges must be resolved in my favour: I would be acquitted.

3) There must be reasonable and probable cause…

4) A prosecution must have been malicious…

The 3rd and 4th elements are made out by virtue of the fact that there was no reasonable or probable cause for my prosecution. A prosecution for causing 'public nuisance' requires that I do, in fact, cause a public nuisance. The public nuisance in this case was clearly caused by their tactics. There can therefore be no 'reasonable' and probable cause. With regard to the requirement for malice, there was clearly an intention by the officers in this case to act for reasons other than to achieve justice. It is clear that the officers wished to bring my protest to a conclusion and it was quite clear from (the notes of Superintendent Tom Henley) that the road closures should be a 'bargaining tool against me and my cause'. The officers were clearly determined to impact on my rights to free speech in acting as they did.

I'd find out later that the police were listening in on all of my walkie-talkie conversations. I can't actually believe that I didn't realise this at the time but I didn't; to be honest, I hadn't even considered it or thought about it for one second, probably because, whether they were listening or not, it would have made no difference. I was doing what I was doing and had nothing to hide from anyone, which was more than likely the reason I never thought about whether they were listening or not. Ed certainly never mentioned anything about the fact that they would have been listening to all we were saying, either. Maybe it was just one of those rare blonde moments by me!

After this protest and on returning to my house, the front door was in a mess after the police had forced their way in, sometime during the previous week. They had had my computer away, presumably in the hope of finding something incriminating on it for them to be able to dish me out further grief, no doubt.

I soon learnt that Jo was contacted by numerous newspapers offering her up to £17,000 to put her side of the story across as to why she was denying Lauryn and I any relationship and to answer a couple of questions. The two questions put to her were, "Why do you not believe David is a good father?" and, "Why don't you think it is appropriate for him to have access to Lauryn?" Jo failed in taking up any of the offers, apparently on moral grounds (as if she had any), stating that she didn't want Lauryn reading about it in the future and that she was worried what Lauryn would think.

The real and main reason she declined was because, of course, she had no reasonable answers to the two simple questions – she knew and I knew that. The facts were that she'd already made two comments whilst I was doing the protest, such as whether I had fallen off yet and, if she said anything about what I was doing it would all be swear words – for these, she wasn't paid a penny – and this is there for Lauryn to read!

Now, she was being offered £17,000 for a few more words, but didn't have anything constructive to say! The money would have gotten her over her apparent lack of finances problem (that she was claiming to the family court at the time, but there never was any lack of finances issue for her – that was just another one of her hundred-plus lies by now) and helped her in being able to afford a solicitor, which she surely needed, to make sure I didn't get anywhere near Lauryn!

She could have put it aside for the future to help with Lauryn's education. But no, this woman with so much to say in the secret court suddenly had nothing to say in the real (and non-secret court) world. Virtually everything she'd ever said in the courts was easily exposed as the total bullshit it was (were anyone in that system interested enough to think about it or do anything other than giving 'mother' everything she wanted).

And, right on cue, Jo dispensed with her solicitor in the 'family' law case, as she couldn't afford one any more. (This, despite claiming to have 17 people working for her, at the same time stating that the business was going well to the family court and having just refused the easiest £17,000 she ever could have!)

It was now over two years since her nonsensical, inconsistent, contradictory and exposed lies on every issue and matter… but, still, she received total assistance from 'family' law, whilst Lauryn and I were continually failed and abused by them all!

On the 12th November, David Irwin from Cafcass (the Children and Family Court Advisory and Support Service) wrote to me, stating, 'In view of recent events, it is my duty to remind you that matters in the court case regarding Lauryn are confidential. It is specifically not permitted to disclose any documents relating to the proceedings without leave of the court.'

If this parasite with less training than your average traffic warden had any idea how to do his job (that is his duty) properly, I wouldn't have had to have carried out any of my protests. And I was already aware that I wasn't allowed to disclose any documents relating to the proceedings, which I never had.

All my immediate family (apart from Lauryn), November 2003
*Relationships with them all (apart from my Mum), ended over the next
few years because of my battles with the establishment.*

On the 2nd December, I was in court at Kingston, Surrey, where my appeal against the harassment conviction relating to Jo was to take place. I'd sacked my original (mis)representation in the matter and was now being properly represented by my new team, with the inadmissible evidence being used. We hadn't even got to the 'inadmissible' evidence part or halfway through the appeal yet when the judge stated that he was doubtful of Jo's evidence from her evidence in chief, which specifically related to her version of the first matter (of the two required to be convicted of harassment). The first matter was the one that the 'inadmissible' evidence related to, the evidence that proved there was no harassment, that I was telling the truth. Jo was doing as she always had and I was only speaking with her because she was fucking with mine and Lauryn's lives and our relationship.

What sprung to mind at this point was, how could the previous judge who'd found me guilty beyond reasonable doubt have done so, when the appeal judge was stating that he was doubtful of the very same evidence, that the previous judge had convicted me on?!

The judge and the prosecution went off to listen to the 'inadmissible' evidence, the recording of the conversation between Jo and I (on the 15th March) where she'd claimed I'd been threatening and had been abusive to her, but where I'd done neither. After hearing the recording, the prosecution stated that they were not in a position to proceed any further and would not resist if my barrister made an application for 'no case to answer'.

My barrister did that and then the judge said that my appeal was allowed and I was free to go.

And this was the appeal that my previous (mis)representation had told me that there was only a slim chance of having the conviction overturned, and that they strongly advised me not to appeal – in amongst all the other bullshit they'd told me.

As I waited outside the courtroom to thank and speak with my legal team, Jo came out of the court, sobbing. That brought a rare smile to my face, her actually being a bit upset, for once. She was sobbing about being caught out, for being exposed that day for the liar she was. She may well have been thinking that her fucked up game of denying and destroying Lauryn and I was coming to an end, but she had no need to worry about that one... 'family' law was on her side, regardless of any facts or evidence from the criminal court system, as I was all too aware of!

Even though a proper court (rather than the farce of a 'family' law court) had exposed her poisonous, lying conduct, it made no difference in the secret court system. It was as if all in the family court system were overruling the criminal court's decision to have found me not guilty and to have cleared me. 'family' law continued to treat Jo as if butter wouldn't melt and Lauryn and I like vermin.

Along came another load of discriminatory and biased bullshit from Irwin (of Cafcass) to the family court. He wrote:

'Even before Mr Chick's successful appeal concerning the harassment of Ms Gowens, comprising two incidents was quashed on appeal, he had been in considerable contact with Kingston social services department, alleging that Ms Gowens has been physically and emotionally abusive to Lauryn. He told me the emotional abuse related to the effect on Lauryn of not having had contact with him for so long and that this was Ms Gowens' doing. He said the physical abuse related to Ms Gowens allegedly throwing Lauryn at two months of age. He explained that he had reported the incident to the Guildford social services department. (This alleged incident is mentioned in the earlier report by Mrs Quinn, as is much of the background at that time). After his appeal, it seems to me that Mr Chick intensified his complaints to social services, demanding that the department take Lauryn out of her 'mother's' care at once, now that it had been proved she had lied in regard to the harassment conviction. I am told that the department viewed Mr Chick's constant demands of them as a form of harassment (not another harassment trial, please!) and a waste of their slender resources. Ms Gowens' present view is that there should be no further direct or indirect contact. I believe that Ms Gowens' expression of her distress is genuine and that she would be committed to Lauryn having a good relationship with her father. I consider that Ms Gowens is a sensible woman, trying to do her best for her daughter. My personal experience of Mr Chick is of a quiet menace, quickly escalating into a confrontational attitude, wherein any sensible discussion is impossible. If that is my experience, I must give credence to that of Ms Gowens. It seems to me that a major issue, at the hearing on the 5th January, will be whether any contact should be resumed at the moment. Such contact could, however, only occur in the face of Ms Gowens' clear opposition, with the possible risks to her health and safety about which she is fearful. My view is that the court should give considerable weight to Ms Gowens' views (which I consider to be valid) especially given her role as Lauryn's sole carer, without any positive contribution from Mr Chick. I consider that it is essential for Mr Chick to demonstrate at the next hearing that he can take a more reflective and balanced view of the situation before contact could take place.'

Drop dead, Irwin, you're beyond sick.

Lauryn turned three on the 15th December. It was now nine months since there had been any contact between us – thank you 'family' law system and 'mother'. You disgusting child abusing freaks.

On the 19th, Barnes and Partners wrote to me telling me that in light of my public comments on national TV they could no longer act on my behalf as there was clearly a 'crisis of confidence'.

I don't recall what I said to upset them and abandoning me

a couple of weeks before my next family hearing wasn't ideal, but it didn't really matter as they were never of any help, pretty much like all solicitors for dads in these courts. Whether I have a solicitor or not, we still get shafted when the 'mother' acts, as certain ones do.

My next move was to write to Critchlow, the main abuser in charge of our family case. Amongst other things, I wrote, 'My daughter and I have had no contact for over ten months now. I now request that this case go to the High Court and that you be removed from this case. You have all abused mine and my daughter's basic human rights and I hold the whole scandalous 'family' law system accountable.'

Within weeks of my sending this letter, on top of my protesting, Critchlow was no longer 'conducting' our case, as it was moved to the highest court in the country, The Royal Courts of Justice. His two years of abuse to Lauryn and I was now at an end.

Now conducting our case would be the President of the Family Division, the highest judge in the country at the time, Judge James Munby (now Sir).

Without my protesting, our case would have stayed where it had always previously been – the abuse to Lauryn and I would have no doubt gone on for many more years and we may well not have been having any sort of relationship with each other until she was 10, 14, 18 with what Critchlow had been doing, based on what had happened over the last couple of years. At any rate, things hadn't been progressing due to his total abuse.

So, my protests definitely helped in getting us back together a lot sooner than we would have been, without me having done so. But just why should anyone ever have to risk their life (hundreds of feet in the air) and liberty once, let alone five times, in order to see their own child that they should never have not been seeing for one second in the first place, as all the 'real' evidence clearly showed?

What the fuck is it all about and why the fuck are 'family' law being allowed to cause so much damage, pain, destruction and deaths?

We all know that money is the root of all evil, as the saying goes…

Is it really all only about making the judges, lawyers, barristers and all involved in this barbaric system wealthy, at the expense of us dads, our children and our lives?

7: Public nuisance? No, a humanitarian service

On the 10th January, I was invited to Channel 4's political awards, having made the top five, which was voted for by the viewers, in the category of 'the most influential person in British politics in 2003'. For that to have happened, quite a lot of people had seen through all that my protest was turned into. It was pretty weird, especially considering I'd never voted in my life or had previously any interest in politics, for Gemma and I to be sat at the same table as Richard Wilson (Victor Meldrew) and Ian Hislop.

It was towards the end of April when my ex-sister-in-law, Allison Reed, entered the equation.

She worked as a children's and families' psychiatric nurse, which you'll probably find somewhat concerning as you read on.

She suddenly had an issue with the fact that her three sons (my three nephews) and I were texting each other, after there having been 'no official' allegations or issues about anything to do with our relationships from her ever before!

After I'd sent a text message in the form of a reply to one of my nephews, she used one of their phones and replied, 'Leave us alone'. My nephews (twins aged 11, and the eldest who was 13 at the time) and I had always had a good, close and loving relationship and I wasn't impressed with this sudden, strange and weird message from Allison. So, I replied back to her, 'Are you on drugs, sicko?' For her to then reply, 'Stop harassing us', was a weird one as I wasn't harassing anyone and to that, I replied, 'I will communicate with my nephews as I like; they won't be with you much longer when they realise what you are'.

That was the end of communications between us (for now).

Prior to the first family case hearing at the Royal Courts of Justice, in front of Munby, it was my Spider-Man, public nuisance trial, which began on the 4th May. I couldn't have had a better legal team representing me and was in no doubt that the jury would find me not guilty on the ridiculous charge the authorities were maliciously attempting to prosecute me on, with all the evidence there was of what had really happened. My solicitor was Steve Holliday, who I recently learned is no longer with us – I couldn't speak highly enough of him. He was a great, decent and top (Scots)man. My barrister was Kyri Argyropolous, who was totally on the ball and a top guy also. And there was Nadine Radford, my QC, who also was one top class lady. Gemma came to court with me every day of the trial; she was my rock throughout these years with her help, understanding, love and support.

The jury of five men and seven women were sworn in on the first day. Then, as the case was just about to get underway, the first little problem arose. The judge claimed that it hadn't been pre-arranged or agreed for Nadine to be able to represent me and that she wouldn't be getting paid. This scenario was virtually unheard of previously… it being mentioned, as the case was literally just about to begin. On hearing this, Nadine made it known that, ideally, she'd like to be paid, but if she wasn't going to be (for whatever reason), that she would still represent me and pro bono, if necessary. That was the first minor hurdle overcome in this farce of a trial, thanks to Nadine's generosity and decency. Over the nine days of this trial, all sorts of other farcical bullshit around the prosecution's case would surface.

The prosecutor, Anthony Wilken, claimed that I was a 'maverick' and was solely responsible for the road closures, the extensive traffic jams, the knock-on effects on local businesses and that I deliberately caused all the chaos by repeatedly ignoring police requests to come down and end the disruption.

My behaviour was as 'plain a nuisance, as you can imagine'.

Their case against me was extremely selective, though. Not one of the senior officers involved in the 'incident' were called, so no Gold, Silver or Bronze... and neither were any of the police officers who took the view that the road closures were not necessary.

There was also the police's health and safety 'expert' who was, in fact, not an expert at all and made assertions in his sworn statement that he himself knew nothing about. He claimed Spider-Man could shift the concrete counterbalance weights on the crane, weighing many tonnes – ones that require a crane to shift – when this was clearly nonsense. This made you wonder, if he and the others had been properly informed of things, what conclusions would they have truly drawn, as opposed to being faced with the pressures of a 'fait accompli'?

It wasn't long before Nadine and Kyri started dismantling and exposing the pathetic prosecution case. Literally everything Wilken was coming out with was total bullshit.

Evidence had come to light showing that on day one of my protest, the Metropolitan Police Service negotiators were refusing to attend the scene on the basis that there was no threat to myself or to the public. It was acknowledged that I was not mentally ill and had no history of causing injury to individuals or damage to property. Despite this information (gleaned from prosecution papers), the MPS decided to effect a pattern of road closures to put pressure on me to bring my peaceful, legitimate, political protest to an early close. Within the 'decision log', it clearly recalls that the road closures were a 'bargaining tool' and that 'any future prosecution would be weakened if routes were reopened'.

It was also recorded that Superintendent Tom Henley stated in a handwritten log, 'Climber does not like road closures so should be used as a bargaining tool against you and your cause'. There was, therefore, a clear indication that not only were the road closures being used to put pressure on me, but the officers seemed to be suggesting that such tactics were legitimate to prevent free speech. Another police record stated that Tower Bridge 'could be reopened if required', but that its continued closure 'could help in negotiations'.

It was 20 hours before my protest concluded that all the roads were reopened, which throughout the protest the police had claimed they could not do, on health and safety grounds, until my protest had finished. This was ample evidence that the closure of the roads and hence the public nuisance, was caused not by my actions but by the tactics invoked by the MPS in their attempts to bring my protest to a premature conclusion.

Once the jury retired to consider their verdict, it wasn't long before they came back in with their 'not guilty' verdict on the 14th May, day nine of the trial.

As I left the court, *(see opposite)* I took my jacket off, now able to reveal the messages written on my T-shirt that I'd been wearing the last few days, which said 'family' law fails children and dads' on the front and 'Police spin version exposed' on the back.

Now the truth was out, there was more favourable coverage than there had been during and immediately after the protest.

This was one:

'Spider-Man triumphs over government forces… during the course of the trial police evidence and documents had revealed a police and government conspiracy to discredit his demonstration.'

There was this piece from Glenn Sacks, an American radio host, columnist, commentator and men's rights activist, that's powerful and to the point. He wrote:

'So many activists have worked hard for years and decades to address the many legitimate grievances which men and particularly fathers face. Yet in less than a week, with one bold and courageous act, an uneducated, unsophisticated window

After my first public nuisance acquittal. Southwark, May 14th 2004

washer achieved something which none of us has ever been able to accomplish – to focus the attention of a nation on the greatest social injustice in the Anglo-American world today – the way decent, loving fathers are driven out of the lives of the children who love and need them. The Mayor of London and the police vilified Chick, but the mute agony of Spider-Man, the image of a man so desperate that he would risk his life and risk prison to be with the little girl he loves moved millions. Polls show that Chick is wildly popular. He continues to fight for other fathers, so they will not have to endure what he has endured. When David Chick talks about his little girl I think of the millions of fathers who have been forced out of their children's lives and I burn with anger. I think of my little girl, and burn with anger over the idea – the idea! – that because I'm male my love for my daughter is somehow cheaper, lesser, not as good, not up to par, not as important. I burn with anger over the hatred and vilification our society has poured on fathers over the last three decades. I burn with anger over the idea that my father is somehow lesser than my mother, and not as important. That it's OK to dismiss my father, degenerate my father, disregard my father, disrespect my father, hate my father. Hate my father? Hate MY father? From the time I could walk I would have walked through the gates of hell for my father, and I would still do it today, I would still do it today!'

And this was one of the on-line posts I came across that also said it as it was:

'These police officers actually tried to manufacture a more serious crime from thin air by subterfuge and deception for which David Chick would have had to pay the price. This is dishonest and dishonourable behaviour by the UK police… and bear in mind this is the same police force that lies to the public by issuing phoney sex-assault statistics on a regular basis and which purposely inflames male hatred by exaggerating wildly all manner of aspects to do with abuse in order, presumably, to avoid having to deal with real crimes.

It's worth noting that the information supplied by the police logs exposed these morally corrupt officers for what they were… Untrustworthy, incompetent, manipulative and malicious. These are not the kind of people we want running our police force. They have one desperate man who wants access to his daughter and these scumbags in uniform try to fit him up by attempting to have him blamed for events that were entirely of their own making.

And to those officers who tried to perpetrate this outrageous deception… you should be ashamed of yourselves.

What hope is there for this country if its police are crooked enough to mislead the public about crimes and are devious enough to purposely increase the harm that is done to thousands of ordinary people, just so they can mislead judges and juries into punishing a man much more seriously than he deserves..? Think about that.

These police officers caused tens of thousands of motorists and passengers, to waste millions of hours of their time, at a cost that runs into tens of millions of pounds, simply in order to hurt one man! What the fuck is going on? Who the hell do they think they are?'

Despite my doing everything correct, right, peacefully, lawfully and legitimately, in my battle on behalf of Lauryn and I, I was being denied my child, being maliciously prosecuted, being tagged, being put under curfew and having numerous bail conditions put against me – when none of these things should have been going on and we were not even halfway through their years of abuse to Lauryn and I yet!

With the bail conditions that I'd had against me over the last six months now gone, I could pretty much do anything again now (apart from have any sort of a relationship with my daughter, obviously).

The day after my public nuisance acquittal I carried out

my fifth protest to remind the authorities that I was not to be forgotten, that I wouldn't stop or be silenced in my efforts to expose 'family' law and that I would never give up until Lauryn and I were back in each other's lives. I would not just continue to take the abuse and bullying I had suffered by them for the last 30 months. It was a very brief and minor protest as I walked across Ipswich Town's football pitch during their play-off match with West Ham (that was live on Sky) wearing my Spider-Man hood with 'Family! Law fails children and dads' in black on the reverse of my white top and 'Mothers who use our children as pawns are sick' on the front.

5th protest. Ipswich (v West ham), May 15th 2004

Around this time, my protests had made me a bit of a local celebrity where I lived. Over a few days following the Tower Bridge trial, I'd drive round in my car with the Spider-Man theme blasting, with my hood on. Loads of kids would be smiling, laughing and waving when they saw and heard me... they enjoyed it, I enjoyed it; it was fun and it's nice to be nice and see happy kids, especially after the most depressing and unhappy times I'd been experiencing for too long.

My nephews would see and hear me too and sometimes I'd pick them up on their way home from school, but there was just the one person that was not impressed with my behaviour and complained about my antics to her solicitor and to the police.

It was Allison Reed, my nephews' 'mother' (again!)... The first family hearing at the Royal Courts of Justice in front of Munby was on the 30th June.

I attended with my barrister, but Jo, in her never ending attempts to delay and obstruct, didn't even show up. Munby, unimpressed with Jo's non-attendance (I know how he felt) immediately attached a penal notice, which meant there could be no more ignorance of court dates by her.

He also ordered that the latest Cafcass officer should consider whether or not there should be psychiatric or other evaluations of the 'mother' – not of the father, of the mother.

'At last, some real progress,' I was thinking. 'Shame it has taken two-and-a-half years to get to this stage, especially when everything was plain to see in the first few weeks.'

Elisabeth Major (the latest child abuser) from Cafcass legal, was now appointed as Lauryn's legal guardian, although there was never any mention in her following report as to whether she had considered if there be psychiatric or other evaluations of the 'mother', as Munby had ordered.

At least it wasn't only mine and Lauryn's contact 'order' made by the original judge being ignored now, now Major was ignoring Munby's 'order' too – and the sole beneficiary of both of the failed orders was, you may have guessed it, the 'mother'.

In July, Major wrote a report for the next hearing due in front of Munby. She just followed suit with the similarly incorrect, biased and discriminatory shit that Irwin, her predecessor, had been saying. It was as if Irwin had written it and Major had just signed it off.

It harped on about 'the stress of these proceedings on the

mother, the mother is fearful of the father' and 'if contact is to be re-introduced… and a parental responsibility order would convey status to the father but could produce difficulties…' And then she summed it up saying, 'My immediate concern is that the focus has shifted (my focus never shifted for one second, for coming up to three years) from Lauryn's needs (that Major and her colleagues have abused and violated throughout) to a national interest in fathers' rights for contact.' (Fathers' rights and contact/access rights still only being mentioned… No, it's the whole of the secret 'family' law court system that needs opening up, amending, rewriting and bringing into the 21st century. Equal rights for mums and dads as there are in virtually every other walk of life, remove the institutionalised bias and discrimination and remove the secrecy that's failing and abusing so many children caught up in this barbaric scandal).

July – and back again came Allison; she's just a watered-down version of Jo. She'd never liked me… and the feeling was mutual. Our families had known each other most of our lives as we grew up living a two-minute walk from each other's houses, went to the same schools and were in the same year. She was like a stuck-up prude and when my brother became involved with her, my whole family was shocked, to say the least. My brother went on to marry her and they had three boys; Alex and twins, Sam and Craig, before her affair with a policeman that started in a churchyard whilst he was on duty and led to my brother divorcing her.

Following their break-up, Allison did a certain amount of Jo behaviour – stopping my brother from seeing his kids, generally making things difficult and awkward for them like a small percentage of 'mothers' do…

As for my brother then getting together with the wife of the policeman who had the affair with Allison… pretty much a straightforward wife swap, but in somewhat odd circumstances… It may sound a little strange, but it was true.

With Allison's children's uncle often on TV and in the newspapers around this time, it would have been grating on her. I could imagine my nephews' excitement about their Uncle Dave being in the papers, on the front page of the local papers and on TV and then probably calling each other in to watch Uncle Dave who's on the telly again. Oh, and he's up on trial over Tower Bridge and been found not guilty after his Spider-Man trial, etc.

Allison would have been sick to her back teeth with her kids' admiration for me and for what I was doing (against 'people' like her) and so she decided she'd join the anti-me brigade (sigh), instructing her solicitor, Valerie Boots of Castles in Haywards Heath, Sussex, to write to me.

This was the content of that first letter dated the 19th July:

'We have been consulted by your former sister-in-law, Allison Reed, concerning contact with her children and, in particular, recent behaviour towards them. We understand that you have recently begun to collect her son, Alex, from school once a week, that you have been texting the children and phoning them. Our client does not wish you to have anything to do with her or her children and wishes you to keep away from them. Do not contact the children again. Do not approach the children at school or come anywhere near them. If your behaviour persists our client will be seeking injunctions against you to keep you away. Be informed that she has notified the police about your behaviour. We hope this letter makes the situation clear, but if you are in any doubts as to your rights we suggest you seek independent legal advice from a solicitor.'

Guilty, your honour, but, actually, guilty of what? Being a man, a male, a dad, an uncle, or just for loving my nephews (who loved me too)?

And as for her suggesting I waste more money on another disgusting solicitor similar to herself, in regards to another sick, threatening, abusing, dictating, controlling 'mother' – fuck off.

I've actually a choice here, not like I had concerning the similarly abominable conduct of my daughter's 'mother' – I'd rather be spending my money on my child than wasting it on any corrupt solicitor, as they all are, involved in this system.

The 2nd September was the day of my trial at South East Suffolk Magistrates' Court, Ipswich, for the football match protest back in May. I was found guilty of having entered a designated playing area without lawful authority or excuse. Gareth Davies, prosecuting, said, "He did it in an entirely peaceful manner. There's no suggestion he attempted any form of violence. We accept he has legitimately held views. We accept he is sincere in his protestations. It's the manner of his protestations on this occasion that we object to."

Magistrate John Fielding said, "We accept he has a right to protest peacefully but Mr Chick walked right into the middle of the game."

When I walked onto the pitch it was during an injury break.

I was off the pitch within a minute of going onto it and, because of my right to protest peacefully (as that was exactly what I did), he could have done the decent thing and found me not guilty, but for whatever reason, decided not to.

I appealed the conviction on the grounds mentioned above, but this was an appeal that failed and would be my one and only conviction in the years from Lauryn's conception through to her turning 18.

I was not impressed with being found guilty for the football match protest, there was still no contact with my baby since March 2003 and, still, 'family' law were totally failing and abusing the only two victims out of Lauryn, the father and the 'mother'. Time for another climb to give these bastards a reminder to get their fingers out their arses and start beginning to repair all the damage they've caused to Lauryn and I in their secret, corrupt and completely fucked up system.

So, ten months on from my second Tower Bridge protest, I

made my final protest to date. It would be my highest and most dangerous protest by far.

I'd done a recce of the next climb a couple of times recently to work out my way in, on and up.

8: Eighteen hours atop the London Eye

Again, I was dressed as Spider-Man, but this time I wasn't on a crane (or a football pitch); I would be appearing on the top of the London Eye.

I had just the one banner with me this time; it was about 2 feet high and about 40 feet long. Hopefully, this time, no-one could be confused about what my protest was about!

On one side, neatly spelled out in my trusted old, black, gaffer tape was 'In the name of the children' and on the reverse was 'Failed and abused by 'family' law'. I trusted they were clear enough to see that my protests weren't just about a father's rights or about contact issues!

On the evening of the 10th September, having packed my banner and other essentials into my holdall, I took the train up to London. Whether I'd get to the structure of the Eye to even be able to attempt my climb, was no certainty. I anticipated it would be nothing like climbing up a crane which was easy to access in the middle of a derelict building site in the pitch-black with no security guards.

Just getting into the area of the Eye and then getting on to it, was a challenge in itself – it was the complete opposite of the crane scenario. There were two or three security guys standing directly outside. The Eye was all lit up and there was a 10 foot barrier to climb over. Even if I got that far, there was no guarantee I'd make it to the structure without being stopped, as that was about another 30 seconds away from the barrier. After walking and loitering around Waterloo for hours, having had a few walks past the Eye to check out where the security guards were and how vigilant they were being, I made my way as discreetly as I could, over to the point where I'd decided to climb in. It was now 4 am on the 11th. After a quick check to ensure none of the security guards were looking, I started the first easy mini climb over the barrier, compared to the second climb that would hopefully be underway a minute or so later. As I jumped down from the Perspex barrier, the strap on my bag broke as I landed. I was using this to put my arms through (so the bag was on my back). It wasn't a great start… or was it in the script?

I had planned to get my bag and belongings to the top of the Eye on my back, leaving both my hands free to climb, but with the strap having snapped I'd now have to hold it in my hand as I climbed, which made the climb to the top all the more awkward.

The noise from my landing alerted the security guys because, as soon as I picked my bag up and started heading towards the structure, one of them called out, "What are you doing?"

I didn't have a prepared response for his question, as I hadn't envisaged being spotted or asked any questions. But my immediate response to him was, "Maintenance," as I hastily continued on my way towards the Eye structure.

I was aware it had been 18 months since I'd last had contact with Lauryn, but I hadn't been thinking what the actual date was. It turned out, totally by coincidence, to be the 11th September. That date probably explained why I was threatened with being shot soon after I'd started my climb around the Eye. It was around 4.30 am when I heard a guy shout from somewhere that I could be shot.

As soon as he said it I shouted back, "Peaceful protest," and continued towards my (midnight) destination. I was taking the very maximum of care in this protest, far more than I ever had to on the cranes, as I knew that one slip of the hand or foot and it would all be over for me – permanently.

I climbed up the inside of the wheel, from where I got onto

it at the '6', up to about the '9' and then I had to get to the outside of the wheel to continue through to the '12' (well, I didn't have to, but it made it a lot easier than going from the '9' to the '12' on the inside of it!) It was about 5 am when I reached the summit. What a view I had for miles in every direction! And the view when daylight came, compared to my previous views from the cranes, was pretty awesome... looking down on Big Ben, the Houses of Parliament and Buckingham Palace, as so many others have experienced from one of the Eye's capsules, but I had to keep one hundred per cent concentration where I was and was clinging on for my life.

A few hours in and some people were making their way up to join me. It was the police rope team guys again, one of whom I'd got to know quite well during my last Tower Bridge protest. It was my old mate, Spoonsey. All joking aside, he was far too good and decent to be working for the police (compared to so many of his colleagues I'd had the misfortune to meet and had had dealings with previously).

It seemed an age from when I'd first noticed them climbing up, to when they arrived near me... well, within shouting distance anyway. They did their bit in trying to talk me into coming down, failed, then headed back down to earth and left me all on my lonesome!

I'd imagined that I might have been able to get on to one of the pods to hopefully be able to relax a bit, rather than always having to be hanging onto something, but they were probably 15 feet away from the structure I was clinging to and were pretty much impossible for me to get onto. There was nowhere to relax or chill, unlike how I was able to in the crane cabs, so it was a case of full-time focus and concentration for the entire duration of my time up there.

The rope team came up to visit me about three times. Once they offered to abseil me down, which would have been nice to do if I wasn't up there for the hugely important reason that I was. I didn't take them up on it for that reason and also because one dodgy bit of rope or any other 'mistake' in the equipment during the abseil down and I'd be dead. So I said, "No thanks, you're alright; I'm good," (knowing I was far more likely to get back down in one piece of my own volition). I'd been in conversation with Barry Pickthall recently, an award winning yachting journalist, respected sportswriter and photographer. Barry called me about 9 am after he'd driven up from near Littlehampton in Sussex where he lived, to take some photos of me for him to provide to the press of this protest. *(photograph overleaf)*

The next time the rope team came up – late in the afternoon or early evening – Spoonsey informed me that it was going to get very windy soon as the tail end of a hurricane was coming across from America. 'Really, Spoonsey,' I thought to myself, 'is that yet more bullshit to try and get me to come down?' But for once, it wasn't.

After the shock of the police having actually told me something that was true for once, I nearly lost my grip on the structure!

When the wind that Spoonsey had quite rightly told me about arrived, it got pretty scary up there, being a tad exposed and nearly 500 feet in the air. It was taking all my strength to just hang onto the structure. I had originally planned to stay up for a few days but that wind actually caused me to abort early. I realised I had to and that was when I decided I'd end this protest. It was becoming that dangerous that I was nearly getting blown off and if that had happened, Lauryn's dad would never have been able to see her again. It had been about 17 hours in total that I'd been up when the wind arrived and was getting really strong. I decided to make the duration of this protest be significant in regards to the 18 months and so held on extra tightly for a while longer. Once the 18 hours was up I began my descent down. In the end, each hour on the Eye

(The other side of my banner) Failed and abused by 'family' law

represented each month of zero contact and zero relationship for Lauryn and I, so at 10 pm I began my descent and by quarter past I reached earth!

On my return to the ground, I was arrested for allegedly being a public nuisance – not that old chestnut again!

I was sure they'd claimed this before and had been proven wrong about it!

This was malicious prosecution and misfeasance in public office number two.

The first two of the four elements of the tort of malicious prosecution, which require that I was charged and subsequently acquitted, were clearly met, as I was both.

As for the other two elements (absence of reasonable and probable cause), it is clear from a consideration of the applicable common law in this case, that there was no basis whatsoever upon which I should have been charged with the offence.

The law can be summarised as follows:

'A person is guilty of public nuisance who a) does an act not warranted by law or b) omits to discharge a legal duty, in the effect of the act or admission is to endanger the life, health, property, morals or comfort of the public, or to obstruct the police in the exercise or enjoyment of rights common to all her Majesty's subjects.'

Although a significant number of people were disappointed that they were unable to ride on the London Eye and the London Eye subsequently did not make the profit that it would have expected from ticket sales that day, neither these people nor the company make up 'a class of her Majesty's subjects'. Whilst my actions may have rendered a group of people unable to visit the London Eye and may have caused the company financial loss, the members of public were able to obtain refunds on the day and British Airways were able to take steps to recoup financial losses. The complaint, related to the London Eye specifically, does not amount to a public nuisance, it related essentially to financial matters. There was no suggestion that the life, health, property, morals or comfort of any of these people had been endangered. Therefore, in order to amount to a public nuisance it must be shown that rights common to all her Majesty's subjects had been obstructed in some way. The opportunity to pay money to visit the London Eye cannot be properly classed as a 'right common to all her Majesty's subjects'. It was not an automatic right that was obstructed. The law of public nuisance relates to rights commonly enjoyed by a class of citizens who are obstructed in some way. No citizen has an automatic right to go on the London Eye. Rather, the London Eye as a commercial enterprise reserves the right to refuse entry. Neither can these disappointed persons properly be described as comprising a 'neighbourhood' or 'local community' whose 'reasonable comfort and convenience had been adversely affected'. Being disappointed in one's hope to visit a paying tourist attraction is very different from being obstructed to the 'exercise of rights common to all citizens'. Only the latter is sufficient to establish a public nuisance. On any reading of the law, my actions did not amount to a public nuisance and there could therefore be no reasonable and probable cause. No person of ordinary prudence and caution could conclude in the light of the facts (which were not in dispute) that I was probably guilty of the relevant offence.

I had at the time of this allegation already been charged and acquitted in respect of an allegation of public nuisance. I was a 'thorn in the side' of the authorities and, as such, given the lack of reasonable and probable cause; the officers acted maliciously in this case to endeavour to ensure that I was prevented from pursuing my protest, as I was of course entitled to do.

Four days after my London Eye protest, another letter was typed up for me at Allison's request and it wasn't to congratulate me about my latest protest! It stated:

'We understand that you have taken to texting the children again. We are instructed you sent each child a text message on the 14th September at 4.07 pm. We have made it clear that our client wishes you to leave the children alone and does not want to hear from you.

(and in capitals) LEAVE OUR CLIENT AND HER CHILDREN ALONE.

The police have been informed about your behaviour and we hold instructions to issue injunction proceedings against you should our client or the children hear from you or see you again.'

Injunction threats again… I still hadn't received the one that was threatened back in July!

Something that summed this woman up in one was her reply to me following the message I sent to my nephews. This was my reply to the three of them asking how I was after my protest on the London Eye:

'Eye'm all right, Spider-Man.'

Allison then texted me, 'Just because you have no contact with your own daughter, don't ruin your brother's.' (I assume she meant to add 'lives'). No, she meant it in regards to his 'contact with his children'.

To me, and I would probably imagine to any normal, rational human being, this was a blatant threat to further abuse her children's contact with their father if I didn't do as she wished and was dictating to me via her solicitor in ending all relations with my nephews.

What a lovely children's and families' psychiatric nurse!

Another example as to why so many have psychiatric problems in the first place – when you have psychiatric nurses behaving like that!

My nephews were well aware by now of much of what was going on between their 'mother' and myself and so was my brother. My nephews all produced handwritten and signed letters (that I have on video). They were all along the same lines and this is one:

'To whoever it concerns. I am writing against the injunction for David Chick not to see us (Alex, Sam & Craig Reed). I want to see my uncle but my mum Allison Reed says he's a bad role model because he's protesting to see his daughter. My mum says she doesn't care how much the injunction costs. The courts say 'we serve in the best interests of the child', I think that's pants, they never listen to the dads or the children. These are my interests, I would love to see my uncle David Chick, I want to see him again because I love him.

I NEED TO SEE MY UNCLE AGAIN.'

Me and my nephews, Alex, Sam & Craig, 2004

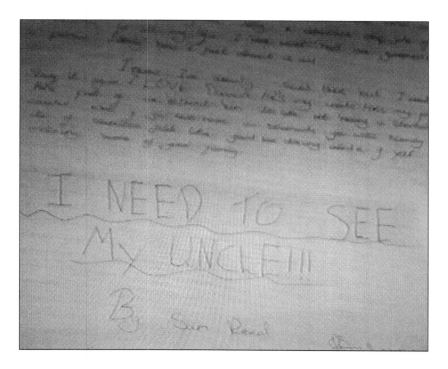

Sam's letter wishing to see me, and against his 'mother', September 2004

My nephews had even put me in their phones under a different name in their attempt to not let their 'mother' know we were contacting each other.

Word came through that an injunction was to be delivered to me and so I arranged with my brother to be round at my house with the boys one morning, hoping it would turn up while they were there. With all the sick games being played out against me, this was hopefully going to be a bit of an awkward one for the injunction deliverer, were it to arrive telling me I couldn't see my nephews if they were with me at the time. I had a cameraman friend present who would video goings-on this day. No injunction actually was to arrive, following all the threats that one would, but my guy did get video footage showing much, including what turned out to be the last ever contact between my three nephews and I – our hugs and kisses goodbye that day, but I didn't know it would be our last ever contact at the time. No daughter and now three nephews also gone from my life (when none should have been – and all due to 'family' law).

Later that day, the police arrived to arrest me within minutes of me speaking with them on the phone. We'd just agreed that I'd surrender for arrest in a few days' time regarding these harassment claims. They'd literally just missed me by seconds though; I wasn't in when they arrived. They were told I wasn't home, but they still searched the house looking for me as my guy filmed them, waking Gemma in the process who was in bed asleep as they searched our bedroom.

The injunction never materialised. It wouldn't have achieved what the authorities required as I would need to be arrested and charged with an offence in order for the police to put the 'illegal' bail conditions against me that they were to be told had to be put in force.

If they had thought about things and done their job 'sort of' properly, they'd have put these 'required' bail conditions against me when they charged me over my London Eye protest a week earlier. But because they hadn't, they needed to go through with this latest false harassment farce of a case… that was no more a case of harassment than the one regarding Jo that they ran against me.

I agreed to surrender for arrest at 4 pm on the 22nd September. I had my solicitor with me, Bruce Clark, from Guney Clark & Ryan, Stoke Newington. We weren't aware at the time that an interoffice memorandum from someone high up in government had been sent to Crawley police station, in Sussex, where my interview was to take place.

It stated: 'Please don't let him leave custody without imposing the bail condition *(banning me from Brighton and Hove with immediate effect, through to 5 pm on the 30th September, which was the duration of the Labour Party Conference).* If the custody sergeant or solicitors are causing problems please seek advice from Superintendent Sloan.'

Following my interview, the two interviewing officers implied there was no case of harassment but at the time they said this they were obviously unaware of the memo.

They left the interview room stating that they would get it kicked into touch, that they would be back shortly and I'd be on my way. Hours passed and eventually I was informed that I was going to be charged... and so the bail conditions, the reason for this whole process, were now possible to put against me.

As for not allowing me to go to Brighton (or Hove) where they feared I might have been planning to do another protest, I was never planning to do anything there as they were probably already more than aware – with Special Branch having been monitoring my calls, texts and e-mails for many months due to my political protests and events carried out by others on the same issue around this time.

This was malicious prosecution and misfeasance in public office number three.

I was subjected to a number of bail conditions which would not have been inappropriate had the matter actually warranted a charge. I was also subjected to an entirely inappropriate condition:

'With immediate effect, not to enter the city of Brighton and Hove unless pre-arranged with Sussex police up to 5 pm on 30th September 2004.'

It was clear from the custody record that this case was reviewed at the highest level (notwithstanding the fact that it was a minor allegation of harassment). There were two superintendents involved. The custody sergeant was clearly unhappy with their involvement and sought the support of Inspector Atkins, the duty inspector. The allegations against me did not warrant a charge. They were minor in nature and the evidence weak, part of which were subsequently 'lost' by the police. However, I was charged not in order to achieve a conviction but to enable Sussex Police to impose bail conditions in relation to a wholly unrelated matter, which they otherwise would not have been able to do. Their aim was clearly to prevent me from exercising my right to protest at the Labour Party Conference. The actions of the officers in this case amounted to misfeasance in public office. The officers (primarily the two superintendents involved) knowingly exceeded their powers by influencing junior officers to charge where they would not otherwise have charged and thereafter abused their power to insist on wholly unnecessary and unrelated bail conditions.

The four elements of the tort were clearly met:

1) I was charged;
2) I was acquitted;
3) There was an absence of 'reasonable and probable cause';
4) The police acted maliciously.

The first two elements were beyond dispute.

'Lack of reasonable and probable cause' – It was clear from the outset that the allegation was minor in nature and the evidence was disputed. The officers indicated at the outset that this was a case that they did not anticipate proceeding with. It was clear that somehow, notwithstanding the fact that the interview was concluded after 'office hours', not one but two superintendents became involved. It was the influence of these officers that led to a charge where there would clearly otherwise not have been one. The police 'lost' evidence that went to the heart of this case but notwithstanding that the police and Crown Prosecution Service (CPS) insisted on continuing with this allegation.

'The police acted maliciously' – It was entirely clear the

police acted maliciously in this case. I was arrested for a minor 'domestic' allegation of harassment. However, I was known to the police as a high profile campaigner exposing the failings and abuse of the 'family' law system and on behalf of children's and fathers' rights. The 'allegations' spanned a period between April 2004 and September 2004. The complainant contacted police early in the proceedings, however, the police only acted on the 16th September 2004 after my London Eye protest, less than a week earlier. I was arrested, charged and subjected to wholly inappropriate bail conditions and thereafter the allegations were pursued vigorously. The officer's motive was something other than a desire to bring me to justice for the alleged harassment offence and was motivated by a desire to ensure that they could impose bail conditions to prevent me from attending the Labour Party Conference. The CPS would not have been provided with this evidence which suggested there was another motive for my being charged and therefore were prevented from making the necessary independent judgement. The charge was thereafter maintained, in an effort to deflect any criticism of the original decision. I was subjected to a prosecution which extended from the 16th September 2004 to the 31st October 2006 – a period in excess of two years – and this charge resulted in the termination of all relations between my nephews and I, and myself and their father/my brother).

Majorly pissed off with yet more abuse of power, I organised for some posters to be printed informing the public just what had happened at the police station and pinned them to trees and telegraph poles in and around my local area, which read as follows:

'Police and politics collude to ban Spider-Man, Dave Chick, from appearing at the Labour Conference in Brighton. Senior police were accused today of taking part in a political conspiracy to ban protester dad, Dave 'Spider-Man' Chick, from staging a headline-grabbing demonstration at the Labour

Party Conference in Brighton. Chick, the children's and fathers' rights protester, who staged an 18-hour protest on the London Eye earlier this month dressed as the comic book hero, was arrested last Wednesday and charged with harassing his ex-sister-in-law. He was finally released by police after having to agree to bail conditions banning him from entering the seaside town until the 30th September. His solicitor, Bruce Clark, said, "It is clear to us that police imposed the bail condition at the behest of someone outside of their authority, probably from the special branch or an intelligence service acting on instructions from someone within the government. To politicise the alleged offence in this way is totally unlawful and a breach of Mr Chick's human rights. The evidence against Mr Chick was flimsy to say the least. This certainly appeared to be the view of the interviewing officers. After the interview, they said they would return in ten minutes. They returned nearly two hours later with a very different perspective. We suspect they had spoken to senior officers who sought direction from the Special Branch, a senior government department or both. Mr Chick was also charged with harassing his former sister-in-laws three sons, aged 11–13. He said, "I have a positive relationship with my nephews. They have texted me and I have texted them back. They have asked me to pick them up from school, for example. They also texted me about the London Eye protest. Then I get a text from my ex-sister-in-law saying that if I contacted the boys again, she would stop them seeing their father, who is my brother. Their marriage broke up because of her affair with a policeman. I have had no other contact with her. This whole business is so obviously a political ruse to keep me away from Brighton, to prevent the possibility of a demonstration affecting media coverage of the Labour Party Conference." Mr Chick is due to appear at Haywards Heath Magistrates' Court on Thursday the 30th September. Last November he staged a Spider-Man demonstration on Tower Bridge that lasted for six days. He was later found not guilty of public nuisance charges.'

Poor Allison was most unimpressed with my mini poster campaign and soon had her solicitor contact the police with the following:

'We understand that Mr Chick came before the Haywards Heath Court on 30th September and the case was adjourned to 21st October with bail conditions in the meantime preventing any contact directly and indirectly with our client and her children and banning him from coming within 100 yards of her house and the children's school. We have been told that an s39 order was made.

Unfortunately this has not stopped Mr Chick from harassing our client further by putting up in Burgess Hill, Hassocks and near our client's place of work, posters, a copy of which we enclose. The first of these was found by the author on Saturday last in Burgess Hill in the High Street attached to a tree outside Superdrug with drawing pins. There were others on other trees. Two more were found this morning in Hassocks by the children near their school, others being seen on trees leading down from the station and near our client's place of work, Larchwood Children's Unit near the Princess Royal Hospital, Haywards Heath. The two this morning had been placed overnight as they were not there yesterday.

It seems that Mr Chick cannot stop his harassment and is intent on continuing to annoy. The posters clearly identify our client and her children and it appears are in breach of the s39 order as the posters were put up after the order was made.

Please be kind enough to pass this letter and the copy poster on to the CPS to add to their file. Perhaps you would also be so kind as to inform us what action if any you are taking given the content and timing of the posters.'

On the 3rd December, I had a meeting with Lauryn's recently appointed Cafcass legal guardian, Elisabeth Major. As always, I recorded the conversation and below contains some of our exchange that day:

(As I was showing her a previous report she'd written).

Me: This is actually your writing now, 'the mother is fearful of the father'.

EM: Mmm…

Me: There's categorical proof that she is not.

EM: Well, it's difficult to judge it, because she's stating she is *(There is numerous indisputable evidence showing that Jo was never fearful of me… but it's difficult to judge according to this expert legal guardian because Jo had been stating she was… How does that make it difficult to judge, when everything else shows that she's clearly never feared me at all?)*

Me: Have you ever known anybody to be fearful of someone for them to say, basically, 'I'll play really fucked up to stop you seeing your own child'. Is that the sort of conduct of someone who is terrified of this man they're saying that to? It's total crap, basically.

EM: Yes.

Me: If you were terrified of someone, if you are alone with someone you're terrified of, a male – would you be threatening them to steal their child out of their life?

EM: No, no, you wouldn't, would you; no.

Me: That's my point. We've got the other case at Bookham (Jo's harassment allegation). We've got both of these on audio tape.

EM: Yes.

Me: I say, 'Why are you doing this to me and Lauryn? I sent you that letter.' Jo's reply, 'I gave it to my boyfriend,' (as she tried to provoke me).

EM: Yes.

Me: Excuse me, I'm trying to talk to my child's female parent.

EM: Yes.

Me: About our child.

EM: Yes.

Me: Trying to have a sensible conversation – 'I gave it to my boyfriend', is that trying to provoke me, or what? Trying to push me over a breaking point, or what?

EM: Mmm, yes.

Me: That is not fear; that is provoking.

EM: Yes.

Me: First one I told you, that is not fear.

EM: Yes.

Me: That is the opposite of fear.

With a legal guardian as unintelligent and incompetent as Major, it's no wonder our children are being ripped from us at such an alarming rate.

Dr Anthony Baker was the 'expert' consultant psychiatrist chosen by Munby to assist in re-introducing Lauryn and I back into each other's lives. Jo was still doing her worst in the meantime; her latest attempt was telling Lauryn that I wanted her to live with me in one of her last-ditch attempts to sabotage our reunion. Put another way, it was Jo telling Lauryn, "That nasty daddy wants to take you away from 'lovely' mummy."

'Lauryn has expressed a view to my colleague that she does not want to live with Daddy and we must assume from this that Mr Chick's residence application has been discussed in front of her,' wrote Baker.

He was inferring that Jo had mentioned something about my residence application to someone and Lauryn had not only 'accidentally' overheard the conversation, but realised it meant I wanted her to live with me. So what he states, that he allegedly assumed was total garbage, as Jo told Lauryn about me wanting her to live with me in yet another attempt to mess with her head worry and frighten her, and in the hope it would result in Lauryn not wanting to see me.

More emotional and psychological stress being inflicted on Lauryn by the 'mother', that neither Baker or Major acknowledged, or thought was wrong in any way or cared in the slightest about Jo saying that to Lauryn.

There couldn't be a more blatant example of parental alienation, a most disgusting form of emotional child abuse that's still not acknowledged by the UK 'family' law system to this day, despite it being recognised as exactly that in various other countries.

I was more than well aware of parental alienation syndrome over 18 months before now, as my banner on this abuse crime referred to in June 2003.

At last, came the day I'd been waiting 21 months for – the 7th December was the day I'll never forget. This was the day Lauryn and I would have our first contact since March 2003. As excited as I was to see my little girl after all this time, I was also apprehensive and nervous about how it might go, considering all the stuff Jo had no doubt been trying to poison Lauryn's mind with in her attempts to turn her against me and sabotage our reunion.

9: Hi again my little princess after 21 months

Was I given any support, advice or anything leading up to this day, by Baker & Duncan? This was not just any little regular meeting between daddy and daughter after a few weeks or a few months of absence from each other's company. You might have thought there would have been, but no, there wasn't – nothing at all.

But I didn't actually need anything from them. I only needed to be my natural self as I always was with my daughter and we would be fine.

They did tell me, however, that our first meeting would be video recorded for them all to be able to see how it went and for the 'mother' to be able to view it, also. Why they even told me it was being videoed, I don't know. It didn't help or make anything about it any easier for me. But then again, so much throughout these years was pointless and/or impossible for any normal human being to understand!

So, on top of the pressure there already was with the near two-year gap in contact, etc, there was now the added pressure that everything to happen and everything I said or did would be scrutinised by all.

As for Jo also being allowed to watch what happened when I was with my little girl after all she'd done and continued to do – that left another one of those disgusting tastes in my mouth.

For the first few minutes after Lauryn entered the room, she seemed scared and apprehensive about being present with me, which was totally understandable and she was also half-hiding behind the woman who'd brought her into the room.

But five minutes later she was right next to me and we were

playing a game as she began to relax and, before long, I was making her smile and laugh. I had wanted to give her the biggest hug and kiss the second I saw her and throughout every minute we were with each other over that hour, but I knew with all that had happened, that was something I just couldn't do right now.

We had our hour together this day, and Lauryn, still a week short of her fourth birthday, knew very early on this day that I was not the monster mummy had been making me out to be and that I was her daddy who'd always and only ever been nice, perfect and loving with her. When the hour was up she even gave me a kiss and cuddle to say goodbye and a wave as I left the room, which was amazing by her, with all she'd been subjected to and had to deal with throughout the last three-quarters of her life.

It was still killing me that her 'mother' and 'family' law had done all this damage and abuse to my totally innocent little princess over the last three years… and it wasn't over yet by a long chalk.

In his report about our contact that day, Baker wrote that I had worked carefully with Dr Petch-Hill to establish an atmosphere of calm, of co-operation, of gentleness. It brought Lauryn into direct 'interactional' contact with me in a way that was extremely positive for us both.

He continued to say that Lauryn waved goodbye to me when I left and that she also complied very easily and in a relaxed way with my request for a kiss and a cuddle to say goodbye. 'There was nothing about this contact, which was in any way concerning on the part of Lauryn or Mr Chick.

'Mr Chick was contained and containing, was entirely appropriate with his daughter, not rushing her, not crowding her, giving her space and, in my view, dealing with her very sensitively.'

As always between Lauryn and I, it was all perfect, positive and appropriate with no concerns; I was gentle and sensitive, etc, but Baker & Duncan would drag this out at a snail's pace over the next 18 months, raking in as much money as they possibly could along the way, whilst not even managing to keep to the snail's pace timetable they were supposed to.

Then there were more incompetent and idiotic quotes from Major:

'I think Lauryn's perception of 'her other daddy' is that he has probably been something of a nuisance to people. *(As if any four-year-old would think anything along the lines of their daddy being something of a nuisance to anyone!)*

'Mr Chick, for his part, is attempting to create a real life romance for himself and Lauryn that in the cruel separation brought about by the mother, the father went to extreme lengths to win justice for the child. (I wasn't just attempting, I was forced into attempting to have the normal relationship that I should always have had with Lauryn, which was brought about by the 'mother' initially but more so and far worse by 'family' law, as they completely backed the 'mother').

Ms Gowens 'says' she could easily tolerate and facilitate contact between Lauryn and Mr Chick. *(She says... 99% of all she says is 'you know what' though!)*

'She does not think that Mr Chick poses any particular risk to Lauryn.' *(So what have the last three years all been about?!)*

With Jo finally admitting this for the first time, as well as the 'experts' stating how extremely positive and fine all had been between Lauryn and I following our re-introduction back into each other's lives, why did Baker & Duncan keep us in this system for another 18 months, before allowing us the normal relationship we should have always had and could have resumed long before we would?

No doubt him raking in around £20,000 was the main reason.

Baker also wrote, 'The child would be best placed with the father if the mother has maliciously, deliberately and purposefully created a web of lies, in collusion with her parents, to create a situation in which Mr Chick has been deliberately excluded from Lauryn's life, then the court may conclude that this is tantamount to very serious emotional abuse which would warrant a child's removal and placement with the father.' This is exactly what had happened and was clear to see within the first two months or at any other point throughout these years, if any of them had any interest in what was best for the child. It was 'family' laws' complete failings, ignorance and condoning of all that Jo had been doing that resulted in the years of abuse... but still this expert doesn't mention anything about 'family' laws' 'very serious emotional abuse'... only Jo's!

And as if they were ever going to admit they'd got everything wrong for the last three years anyway...

And the final line in his report said, 'Ms Gowens has already experienced a media invasion as a result of Mr Chick's actions and I think that a repetition of such an experience for her or her family may create a circumstance in which the criteria for contact which I have set out may no longer be achievable or even reasonable.'

So, if I don't do as I'm told, you'll remove Lauryn and I from each other again! More sick threats and abuse... will it ever end?

And low and behold, a letter was sent to Munby by Jo, emphasising that very same sentence in Baker's report, 'I think that a repetition of such an experience for her or her family may create a circumstance in which the criteria for contact which I have set out may no longer be achievable or even reasonable.'

This 'expert' organisation instructed by the court with assisting in getting me and Lauryn back together ignored Jo's continual attempts to damage us, her obstruct and delay tactics and failed to even keep to Munby's timescale as things ran weeks late, then months late and then it was two months behind schedule...

And Elisabeth Major chirped back up with the following in her next report:

'The 'mother' struggled to think that she could make weekly meetings, as proposed by Dr Baker (that had been decided was best for Lauryn) but could make fortnightly ones. Every week would be hard for her as it wiped the afternoon away.'

So, once again, what was in Lauryn's best interests was changed to what was in the 'mother's' best interests. Our relationship would now go at 50% of the rate it should have been going, as was suggested by Baker and with everything taking twice as long as it should have. And as for Jo's line – 'it wiped the afternoon away' – she'd already wiped away Lauryn's whole relationship with me (with the assistance of all in 'family' law) for the last three years. It continues:

'Mr Chick expresses himself very clearly in his deep bitterness towards Ms Gowens in saying that he was a happy man whom she had robbed of all he valued. He had everything anybody could want, especially his status as a father. He maintained contact with Lauryn, it was going well, he has videos to prove it. He feels so bitter because Ms Gowens has taken away from him his home, his working life, his sense of family, his feelings of self-respect and he believes that she has set out deliberately to hurt him. In addition to his own losses, he expresses himself in a way that indicates he identifies very strongly with Lauryn, claiming that Lauryn is damaged and hurt by her mother's action in preventing her from having a relationship with the father who loves her. He speaks of Lauryn being damaged by her mother's abuse.

'Ms Gowens' refusal to allow him contact in defiance of court orders has become in his mind a serious crime and further evidence that she is an abusive mother. He insists that she has demonised him to Lauryn who once referred to him as 'her nasty daddy'.

'Mr Chick fails to see that his manner of protest is unlikely to bring about justice on anyone's terms. Like the Spider-Man hero-icon that he seeks to emulate, he himself becomes regarded as a pest and a nuisance (only to 'family' law and the authorities) and yet, it can be seen that his protest in its extreme form is borne out of his sense of impotence and outrage. He gives the impression of being proud of his media image and the impact that he has created in general in drawing attention to his plight with Lauryn as an example of a general systematic injustice in the UK. He has continued his protests – his 'mission' – seemingly putting what he sees as the general good before Lauryn's (seemingly to you, maybe). On the one hand his commitment for all children and fathers is admirable and he has indeed succeeded in his own terms (indeed succeeded in my own terms – I beg your pardon – please explain, you deranged parasite).

'I would hope that as contact continues (at the reduced rate to suit 'mother') he will curtail his activities (or I won't see Lauryn any more) and concentrate on building a relationship with his daughter (who I'd never not concentrated on for one second).

'I believe that the father is genuinely attached to Lauryn *(Brownie point for you, Einstein!),* even though his opportunity to form an attachment to her has been limited *(average of 16 hours of contact per year – limited, so mmm, you could say that!)* His commitment cannot be questioned *(anywhere, ever, so how has any of this occurred?)* He wishes to play a full part in her life *(as I always should and could have)* to the extent of caring for her full-time.

'I recommend that the application for a contact order *(had them before, they're pointless and mean nothing)* be adjourned to the first open date after nine months.' *(Nine months... So much still for minimal delay in cases involving children!)*

Although, previously there would be over a year until a next hearing, so perhaps I should be grateful you've sped things up since then!

Five days after Lauryn turned four, another birthday where we didn't see each other for a second, the court 'ordered' that I now had parental responsibility.

I was told over three years ago that I could have that, in the first letter from Jo's solicitor!

But, as per all other orders, for me, and/or Lauryn, I was still denied the information that having parental responsibility now entitled me to, by Jo and by Major for over another four months!

It was no wonder that Baker & Duncan were keeping this going for as long as they could, for the longer it went on the more money they raked in, of course. As for who was paying them, it was being paid half by Cafcass with the other half being paid by – you may have guessed it – me, with Jo not having to pay a penny.

Talk about progress... In January 2002 when the first contact hearing occurred, Lauryn and I were ordered eight hours of contact per month. Now, fast-forward three years later and we are having just two hours per month. So that's 25% of the amount of contact we 'should' have been having three years ago (not that we ever did), or if you look at it the other way, we're now to have 75% less than we were to have back then.

And on top of this, Baker couldn't even manage to keep to the scheduled timetable agreed by himself and the judge regarding contact for Lauryn and I, with it progressing to unsupervised and then onto overnight stays.

Concerning Lauryn's GP and school information that I'm now officially entitled to, in January, Elisabeth Major wrote to me the following: The mother was not happy for you to have details of the school at present. She is going to discuss GP details and think this over and will let me know. You might like to raise this as an issue in court (in April), or with Dr Baker as well.'

Why is this Cafcass 'legal guardian' of Lauryn doing nothing about me being given this information and doing nothing about the 'mother' denying it to me also? This was potentially for another three months, as the next court hearing wasn't until April!

Another four months of being denied information that I was entitled to know last month.

Again, an 'order' by the court to the 'mother' being ignored by her and Major doing nothing about another 'order' being ignored!

And Jo confirmed it all, stating, 'At present, I will not be providing the details of Lauryn's nursery and GP.'

In April, Baker stated that, 'All the reports of the contact are satisfactory and there is evidence that Lauryn enjoys her contact with her father, looks forward to it and she is renewing a very positive relationship with her dad. Mr Chick's partner has been introduced to the contact and this has gone extremely well. Lauryn herself speaks well of the contact times. Mr Chick is clearly impatient to move things ahead as soon as possible (yes, before I miss out on the whole of my daughter's childhood) to overnight staying contact and to reaching a point where he and Lauryn might (fucking 'might'!) spend prolonged periods together. Thus far, significant progress (best slow it down a bit then, to make some more money) has already been made in accordance with the plan and, from my point of view, this has been achieved with many smiles and no tears from Lauryn.'

Despite everything going extremely well, etc, regarding everything about every contact between Lauryn and I, it would all continue at the snail's pace for another year – which wasn't in Lauryn's best interests at all, only Jo's and all the 'family' law system parasites involved.

With a worried expression on her face, in May Lauryn said to me, "Don't run away with me, Daddy." This was the day we were having our first outside contact, as up until this day our contact had always been indoors. I answered, "I'd never run away with you, darling," and gave her a big reassuring cuddle in my attempts to allay any worries or fears she had.

I asked her why she'd said about not running away with her the next time I saw her and with my recording device on to prove more of Jo's disgusting conduct and abuse to our child, Lauryn replied, "That's what my mummy said." I knew that would have been the only reason for Lauryn having said it to me before she answered. Again, this was yet more indisputable evidence of unnecessary and serious emotional abuse to Lauryn by her 'mother' and more evidence of Jo's never ending sick attempts to make things difficult for us.

In June, Lauryn got a half-brother, Elliott, which Jo had produced with Alan. The latest was that now Jo would try and use the new baby as a reason to slow down any progress with Lauryn and I. Jo told Major, "It is important Lauryn doesn't feel left out with the new baby (what, like she totally had been with her male parent) as visits to the father's home are due to start." She then went on to suggest that this might not be the time and was worried things would go too fast and too far to the overnight stays. Might not, worried, too fast, too far… Please, someone, put her to sleep!

Along came some more information from Major in her next report written in July:

Regarding Baker's contact plan of contacts, 1–4 were to be fortnightly with close management, then 5–8 being short times with Lauryn and I alone and Gemma's introduction. Then 9–12 contacts were to be in a neutral venue and with some time alone prior to the contact supervisor talking with Lauryn regarding contacts and then 13–16 with Lauryn coming to my house.

And she also stated: 'No overnight stays until a major review.' Is that an Elisabeth (shit) Major review?

I'm sure just 'a review' without the 'major' would have sufficed!

Then she wrote, 'This suggested plan means the father might have won the battle but the war was not over.'

Now, what was this reprobate on about? I hadn't won anything as far as I was concerned, I'd lost out on having any sort of relationship with my little girl for all of those most precious years, just as Lauryn had with her dad too... and all thanks to 'family' law!

And as for her using the words 'battle' and 'war'... that's what this whole barbaric and corrupt 'family' law system is all about. They purposely cause and/or assist the battles and wars between the parents, which results in so many cases ending up in the court system for months, even years. It makes a very nice income for everyone involved and 'working' within this most evil heinous and sick secret system.

And she wrote, 'The 'mother' was not happy with an increase in contact in June.' What a surprise! No doubt she was hoping for a decrease, or contact being stopped as she'd done from March 03–December 04, with Major's associates doing nothing about it throughout those almost two whole years!

And in her assessment she wrote, 'Concerns regarding harassment have ceased and the 'mother' has been able to co-operate and put her previous fears behind her' (despite nil evidence anywhere that she was ever harassed; oh, and the fears... the fears of the poor female who threatened to play 'really fucked up' all those years ago, in regards to mine and Lauryn's relationship! She was never in fear of me for one second, as numerous evidence makes blatantly clear). You really deserve a pay rise, Major – you're so awesomely brilliant at your 'job'!

Hold on, there are actually a couple of correct lines from her... 'She can tell the truth and be a human being when she puts her mind to it...' 'It is clear that Lauryn is enjoying renewing her relationship with the father and that contact has progressed successfully and there are no concerns in her father's care during contact.'

It was on the 16th August that another milestone in this whole disgusting saga was to be achieved. This would be the first time since October 2001 that Lauryn and I would have unsupervised contact. Virtually four years had passed since we'd been denied our basic human right to have any sort of a private family life with each other.

It was a lovely sunny day. Gemma and I picked Lauryn up from her mum's house in Chessington, Surrey, and headed straight down to Lancing, Sussex, for a few hours down on the beach together. What an amazing feeling that day was, just being with my baby and without any strangers monitoring us in any way, shape or form.

At the beach with my girl, 2006

Lauryn and her Nanny Chick, 2006

The following month, however, Jo was still being Jo. The practice manager at Baker & Duncan left a message on her answerphone concerning a contact for Lauryn and I.

Jo made out she never got the message, but Janice Caluori, the practice manager, stated there could be no mistake as to Jo having received the message as she left it at the end of Jo's own recorded message when she didn't answer the call.

Janice asked Jo to explain why she'd not contacted the office about this contact that would not happen once more now, because of yet more impede and obstruction by her...

...but did anyone do anything about that? Of course not!

Munby had stated that it would be possible for progress to

reach the point for the father to have staying contact during the school summer holidays, but once again and as per the above, the first staying contact didn't take place on time.

This next milestone occurred on the 8th October. What a day and night! My little girl is finally allowed to have a sleepover at her dad's. How privileged are we!

Nearly four years since all this bullshit commenced. Since I was sleeping in the same house as my daughter since her birth and where and when there was never any real issue anywhere concerning us, we're now allowed an unsupervised sleepover in the same house! It was lovely and amazing to have Lauryn staying with me... when it should have been normal and run-of-the-mill at best, but she should have actually resided with me and would have done had 'family' law done what was in her best interests – as they're supposed to do – BUT DON'T.

Was I meant to be happy and thankful to any of them about it? No fucking way. How could anyone ever be happy or thankful about all the years of abuse?

Feedback from Dr Catherine Humphrys (a colleague of Baker's) to him, was, 'I can say that the overnight stay for Lauryn with David Chick ('her dad' or 'father' would have sounded better here, Dr!) was a great success.' Why ever wouldn't it have been? There is four years of evidence of any and everything concerning Lauryn and I as having always been perfect!

The following weekend, Gemma and I had a blessing at The Courtlands Hotel in Hove. One of the reasons we had a blessing was because her granddad was very religious and, as by now we were planning another half-brother or sister for Lauryn ourselves, we thought that her granddad would be less upset were we blessed than had had no ceremony at all, were our sibling for Lauryn to come to fruition. This was one of the happiest and nicest days of my life and there was no-one better than Gemma to have a blessing with.

There were some very special events in my life of late –

unsupervised contact and overnight sleepovers with Lauryn and my blessing with Gemma. What's going on?

But soon it was back to the regular grind of the last four years-plus, as fast approaching was the latest malicious prosecution trial, Labour Party Conference bail conditions and harassment of my nephews and ex-sister-in-law one.

It was just a week before this trial and some 15 months after my arrest on this 'matter' that the police took a statement from Alex for it!

The main thing that jumped out in his statement was him saying that I'd spoken to a schoolgirl one day and asked her to get in my car, or had offered her a lift.

He could have only possibly come out with that because Allison had got him to say it.

If anything anywhere near as serious had happened or been alleged against me, the police would have been all over me like a rash within five minutes of anyone alleging it happened.

The fact that I was never charged, arrested or even spoken to about that 'incident' was more than confirmation that it never occurred.

As for the police doing nothing about this serious false allegation, when with the press of a couple of buttons they could have seen the alleged schoolgirl incident had never occurred – that's them against me, all over.

It's fine though, we'll let anyone say anything bad or incriminating about Chick, whether it be true or not, if there's a chance it might make things worse for him!

I remember poor little Alex stood in the box as white as a ghost at this trial, looking nervous and scared of everything going on when the trial commenced. How nice of his 'mother' to subject her own son to such an ordeal!

Here was Alex having no real choice or option than to take his mum's side over mine, an uncle he'd always loved and been close to, but whom he'd now been forced to, not only be a witness against, but also that he had to lie to the court in the process.

Whatever the reason, probably because I'm a male, this magistrate (wrongly) found me guilty of harassment. There was no evidence of any harassment by me, just his 'mother's' words. There was never even any evidence to charge me in the first place. I was only charged in order for the illegal political bail conditions against me to keep me out of Brighton whilst the Labour Party Conference was going on.

So, due to a second wrongful harassment conviction, I now had another appeal to go through...

You really need to try and get it right next time... Do you actually know what harassment is, Magistrate?

I do – I've had it from police and the authorities untold times, over decades... as well as the other crimes they do to me directly and cover up by others... and all I can do is just live with it!

I'd politely asked Jo in an e-mail to her, to refer to me as Daddy, rather than David, to Lauryn, as she always had done when I'd heard her speak to Lauryn regarding me.

'Do address u as daddy to Lauryn although have to resist calling you prick to her sometimes,' was her reply.

I didn't bother replying back to that (what's the point!), but I just thought I'd rather be one of them (that I'm not) – than what she undoubtedly is with all she's subjected our daughter to...

In January, Baker prepared his next report. I'd made a suggestion about collecting Lauryn from school, which Baker stated he was in support of at the time.

This was dismissed, however, by Jo's wish that yet again prevailed over mine by the experts. He also suggested that there could be more benefit from continuing the work with Dr Humphrys for a further period of six months.

Further benefit to your bank balance, yes – as for any benefit to anyone else apart from Jo... there wasn't any.

But in his recommendations at the end of his report, he fully supported the principle of the (Lauryn's) school holiday time being shared 50% between Jo and I.

Now, 50% each – how fair and right this actually sounds, for once. A child is basically 50% of each parent anyway… So why, when parents separate, is this not the starting point on everything concerning the future relationships between the child and the parents, never mind whether they're married or not?

It's not that difficult; it's right and fair, the most blatantly obvious way to go about things and reduces the parent with the upper hand/residence of playing any of the disgusting games because of the fact that they're in control and have the power to do so, that had been given to them by this even more disgusting 'family' law court system that needs abolishing and rewriting ASAP (decades ago).

10: Famumily law out of our lives at last

By now, Lauryn had her little brother. He was about four months old when his dad suddenly wasn't in his life full-time any more. I was wondering why he'd split up from Jo so soon after having a child with her, with them having split up in under half the amount of time that I'd managed to stay with Jo following Lauryn's birth.

Regarding Jo now being separated from the fathers of both her children, Humphrys wrote: 'Ms Gowens is struggling valiantly with working and two small children, having separated from her new partner, Alan.' ('New', he was no longer 'new').

Struggling... ahhh, and valiantly... organise her a medal!

But no questions or concerns from them as to why Alan had also 'left' ('left' or 'forced out', more like) this woman and his own child and in less than half the time it took Jo to have our child all to herself...

I wonder why Alan's not with her or his son any more?

Must be another bad male/dad, it can't be Jo's fault or anything she may have done wrong or underhand... surely!

She also wrote, 'Lauryn is happy and blossoming in her father's care' (as always).

Regarding Lauryn's packed social calendar, she wrote, 'This is an area where Jo seems (is) very unwilling to make changes regarding Lauryn's very crammed evening schedule every night, that seems (is) excessive for her age – for which Jo is reluctant to cancel any and lose money.'

This was all still ongoing most blatantly by Jo to deny Lauryn and I any evening contact during the week and with the experts still doing all but nothing about it.

And on parenting issues, Humphrys wrote, 'Mr Chick has a

strong sense of a young child's need for routine and discipline that is consistent and fair. However, as David notes, Lauryn frequently goes into her 'mother's' bed and wants to stay there. She may need reassurance and closeness following the loss of her 'other daddy', Alan, who separated from Jo in October (October, hmm – it was an October we 'separated' too!) causing further disruption. Jo is trying to be firm but also being sensitive to Lauryn's needs (what, just like she was sensitive with her needs to see her daddy?). Meanwhile, Lauryn is now trying to come into David's bed.'

'No dad', 'one dad', 'two dads', 'nasty/monster dad', etc, Lauryn has been so psychologically damaged by her 'mother' and the system that it's no wonder she's confused.

And as for Jo and all in 'family' law who've done all the damage to her… they need locking up, at least, and far worse if I had my way… they're nothing but pure evil.

May – Four-and-a-half years after Jo's attempt to kill mine and Lauryn's relationship, I finally got her back from the system that made the last four-and-a-half years hell happen. Now, finally, we had the unrestricted relationship that we shouldn't have not had for one second.

As well as what was done to Lauryn and I and our relationship, it was impossible for me to work for a living for those five years, as I mentioned earlier, as getting our relationship back was far more important to me than anything else… With the court appearances, Cafcass meetings, solicitor and barrister meetings, conferences, appointments at Baker & Duncan and my protests, etc, these all tied me up on over 150 separate days over those five years. Any employer would lose patience with an employee constantly saying, 'Sorry, I need to be in court again tomorrow'.

Financially, it cost me the equivalent of at least £100,000 in lost earnings in today's money, as well as the thousands I paid out to solicitors, barristers, etc, during those years.

I'd done more than my bit, in my attempts to expose this evil 'family' law system for what it is. Now my main focus would entirely be on making the most of the years ahead with my daughter in my life rather than not in it, as much as possible.

Over the following years, Lauryn and I enjoyed the last two thirds of her childhood together, just like the majority of children and parents do. There was never one problem anywhere with us, just as there never had been. Lauryn was now able to see her other nanny again – my mum – after all those years apart. My mum wasn't that well by now, but she loved Lauryn and Lauryn loved her nanny once she/they were allowed to be granddaughter/mother again.

Gemma was always brilliant with Lauryn from the day they met, and they became really close in no time. We soon got Lauryn her first pet, a little lop-eared rabbit she named Cleo. We'd often go over to my sister's where she'd play with cousin Ryan. They got on great and Ryan would often come to ours to play with Lauryn and have sleepovers. Now, everything was pretty much as perfect as it could be.

One day I managed to speak with Alan, Elliott's dad (and recorded our conversation), as I wanted to find out what had happened. Why had he also now separated from Jo so soon after his son's arrival? We shared small talk for a while and then I asked him, "So, how come you split up with Jo?"

His reply was, "She came at me with a knife." That didn't surprise me one bit.

What a great 'family' law system we have here in the civilised UK!

If all they're doing wasn't being done behind closed doors and in secrecy, none of what had happened to Lauryn and I could or would have happened.

As for their claim that the secrecy is there to protect the children... it categorically and totally isn't and failed to protect my child for nearly five years!

The real secret is that so much is being done that's in the child's worst interests.

That, and the pain of it all, breaks untold dads with many taking their lives to put an end to their hell.

This is on top of the damage being done to the children and the damage being done to society in general with the knock-on effect of what's being done to us and our children, regarding crime, mental health issues, etc.

In October came my final court appearance of this era, which would have been at least the 50th different day that I was in a court between 2002 and 2006. This time it was for my appeal against conviction regarding me having 'harassed' Allison and my three nephews.

Just as my previous wrongful conviction relating to Jo was corrected, quashed and overturned on appeal, this one would also be.

But this whole abuse of power 'case' and the bail conditions related to it, that had lasted for over two years in total, had long before now managed to irrevocably destroy all relationships between my nephews and I and my brother and I... thank you, again, upholders of the law!

It was only to stop another potential protest about 'family' law that this case ever got off the ground. And the result of it all? I'd lost another four members of my family who had also lost me. This 'law really needs re-naming 'Breaking up families law fits much better, or 'Destroying families law or perhaps just change the spelling to 'Fam-ILL-y law, as it is so ill/sick. What is most heinous and scandalous about the secret 'family' law cover-up is that, considering what they did to Lauryn and I for the best part of five years – none of which should have gone on after the first few weeks/couple of months with the evidence of all that there was (is) – then just how many others' children (and fathers who didn't gather the evidence that I did) have been and are being failed and abused in a similar way over recent decades?

This was to be Lauryn and mine's first full year together, finally out of that system that had caused so much pain and damage and without any of the absence from each other's lives for weeks or months at a time.

Gemma and I had a great relationship, we were living together happily and every time we had Lauryn with us, everything was as perfect as it could possibly be. We'd do everything any other parents would do with their six-year-old daughter. We'd go fruit picking, camping, swimming, horse riding, over to the Isle of White or to the beach and park... Having Lauryn back with me meant these years were the happiest and most precious of my life.

Cuddling my girl, 2007

Me, Gemma & Lauryn, 2007

Gemma's parents, Paul and Dot, were as good as Lauryn's grandparents and they treated her just like she was their own grandchild. They doted on her and Lauryn was very fond of them, although she did have a little problem with Paul, which was neither her fault nor his. Paul was brilliant with Lauryn, playing with her, making her laugh and having fun, etc, but he'd only ever get a handshake goodbye, rather than a kiss and cuddle, unlike Dot. I felt quite sorry for him, as he deserved a proper goodbye. No doubt this was a result of all that had gone on in the years when we hardly saw each other. Lauryn had a little issue with men and it was obviously because of what happened to her regarding her other 'daddy' and I and was basically down to what Jo and 'family' law had done to her psychologically. We'd often go down to see Paul and Dot with Lauryn. Gemma's brother, Adam, was brilliant with Lauryn too. His girlfriend at the time, Lauren, was also great with Lauryn; they'd both play with her and had her laughing all the time. And it was a little awkward sometimes with two Lauryns/Laurens around, so one was referred to as Big Lauren and the other as Little Lauryn. And just like with Paul, Adam would only ever get a handshake goodbye from Lauryn, whereas Big Lauren would get a kiss.

During this time, there would still be some not so great and painful stuff sporadically happening, but that's part of life when it's sporadic... and nothing could ever have hurt as much as what happened before. It was this year that Gemma became pregnant and this was the most amazing news I'd heard since Jo announced the same some seven years before. I'd already decorated the spare room for the impending addition to our little family and Gemma was going to be the perfect mum to have a child with. As I said, she was absolutely brilliant with Lauryn from the day they met.

But not long after Gemma found out she was pregnant, she was in pain and a few days later our baby was no more when she suffered an ectopic pregnancy. Talk about life dealing out a nice hand... or being fair.

It still makes me sick to this day when I think how Gemma will never be able to have her own child or be a mother to her own child, especially when she's such a loving, caring and decent human being, when you consider that there are others who don't even deserve to have a child (let alone children), with certain things they do and the way they treat and abuse their own children.

In 2007, Matt O'Connor, the founder of Fathers 4 Justice, had his book published. As for the lies he wrote in it concerning my protests and I, they showed him along the same lines as the mums and those in 'family' law who do this stuff to our children and us.

None of my protests were anything to do with him or his organisation in any way, shape or form, as he admitted at the time during both my Tower Bridge protests in the various TV news clips he appeared on and in the press. At the time, he even stated, "Mr Chick is supported in his protest by Fathers 4 Justice. His action was not an official F4J protest, it's an unofficial action, but we support him fully."

But now, four years later, he was claiming my Spider-Man Tower Bridge protest was one of his and that he was the mastermind of it!

He was either telling the truth at the time or in his book... it obviously can't be both... and from the evidence there's no difficulty in seeing which was the truth!

There were never any PR instructions to me from him as he also claimed he gave me.

As you know, I agreed to take his banner up with me when it was suggested as, after all, we were fighting the same evil and because we were (supposed to be) on the same side.

I hired my Spider-Man suit from a fancy dress shop in Haywards Heath, Sussex, (and I still have the piece from my local paper of the lady jokingly asking me if she could have it back) which he claimed he provided me with.

I carried everything up to the top of the crane as I did on all my protests, despite yet another false claim he made that some of his members were involved in getting my stuff up to the top.

And as for him saying I could have made a small fortune following my protest... I didn't care about making any sort of fortune, big or small. I was doing it for my small child/our children and dads. Neither money nor fame came into it with me – shame he can't say the same.

I was doing all that I was doing, which I'd begun before his F4J had even done one direct action (their first being in December 2002), already having carried out my first two crane protests (August and September 2002), as I wanted to see my small child. I was also doing my utmost in exposing the secret and barbaric system stealing us and our children from each other's lives (often for no justified reason) to as many as I could.

My behaviour cost them support, he claimed… My second Tower Bridge protest actually launched his organisation around the world and got him and his brand thousands of members, so he told me himself in the weeks after MY protest.

He also conveniently failed to mention that I donated £2,000 from the money I got for my exclusive in the Daily Mail, to his organisation.

He wasn't happy with me, having done more than him on the issue and my being above him (not only literally) all over the Internet, rather than his organisation.

To change that and within six months of my Spider-Man Tower Bridge protest, he organised his headline-grabbing attack on the Prime Minister, after someone managed to get a pass or two into Parliament, followed by a split second throwing of a condom containing purple powder.

Not exactly a great way to act and with minimal thought and duration, but obviously headline-grabbing as it involved the then Prime Minister.

Unfortunately for F4J, that was followed four months later by another headline-grabbing stunt involving the Queen. The guy who did this one was laughing and joking with the authorities while he stood on the little balcony at Buckingham Palace for a few hours; it was basically what O'Connor was turning this most serious issue into by now – a joke. And this, after I'd made six such serious and peaceful protests in a non-violent and lawful way and had made progress in making people aware during those two years. I didn't throw anything at anyone and there was no laughing or joking about with the authorities by me on any of my protests.

And after stunts involving the Prime Minister and the Queen, where else was there to go?

Soon after, F4J pretty much fizzled away and had changed nothing – you hardly hear anything about them any more.

I've no doubt he had good intentions when he set out, but it soon became all about him.

He believed he could change the law in a few years, which he obviously never achieved and enjoyed having the power and control overall in his organisation. But, sadly, he soon lost focus on what the real and original goals and objectives were.

He couldn't control me or tell me when to or when not to do anything, as he tried to on my second Tower Bridge protest. Ed told me O'Connor wanted me to leave it a few days – no doubt it wasn't an ideal time for him to be able to get there to do all his publicity stuff, but I did as I'd always done – my protest – exactly where and when I decided I would.

And as for his laughable story about having an epiphany whilst standing on Waterloo Bridge in 2001, claiming that was when he decided to have dads climbing bridges, rather than jumping from them...

As if anyone has an epiphany about doing something that they're terrified of doing and would never do themselves. It's on record that he has a major fear in climbing anything and he never has climbed anything, apart from a few stairs (or, perhaps, to get into his cot).

Odds on, his 'epiphany' was the drink talking again.

And if his epiphany was real or true, then why was it that there were no protests or climbs on anything from his organisation until October 2003 (after he'd seen what I'd done and was doing, with him having been present at and all over my first Tower Bridge protest in June 2003)? And even then it wasn't a bridge that was climbed by them, it was just a roof!

If he had done as I had been doing (or followed his epiphany – he never had!) and climbed cranes regularly and all over the country over the following months and years, as I'm sure he could have arranged with the thousands of members he had, then I'm sure there would have been a lot more progress and possible change in the sinister 'family' law system long before now... What a massive missed opportunity, going the route he went, so soon after I'd raised much awareness on the issue.

The truth, that he doesn't even have to admit, as I have the proof and evidence in front of me to back what I say, is that he only thought of protesting in the air – on roofs, bridges and on top of cranes – after hearing and seeing what I'd done up in the air on the cranes and on/by Tower Bridge.

Prior to this, all he'd organised was a couple of things at ground level... storming a court and a parade around the streets of London.

So, pretty much every word he said in his book about my protesting strategy, his alleged epiphany and me was all Billy bullshit. I wonder how much else in his book also was!

He's admitted that the problems he had seeing his own kids related to how he was at the time – because of his drinking problem.

By the time he set up F4J, his difficulties in seeing his children had been sorted out. I did all I was doing on this issue alone and at the exact same time I was having to deal with my daughter having been ripped away from me and I, unlike him, hadn't a drink problem or done anything whatsoever to have deserved to have been having the nightmare experience that I was.

Stabbing the guy in the back and worse, that had done so much for the cause and for his organisation!

11: My sectioning plotted so I'd miss Lauryn's 18th

For Lauryn's 7th birthday in December, Gemma and I were hoping to surprise her with a trip to Lapland. Gemma e-mailed Jo to ask if she would allow us Lauryn's passport, because if she wouldn't it would be a waste of time and money arranging anything. A few e-mails went back and forward with Jo basically taking the piss out of our daughter and I (as always).

'I require more information regarding your proposed trip,' she wrote, and 'country you are intending to travel to, dates, times and proposed method of travel, details of where you are looking to stay whilst you are abroad.'

Fucking skank, we never were allowed Lauryn's passport by her and so Lauryn lost out once more. I wouldn't even give her the satisfaction of declining us her passport again after that. Any future holidays for the foreseeable future for Lauryn and I would only be in the UK.

What a lovely woman, 'mother', human being – and as for the system assisting that, abusing and failing Lauryn and I for nearly five years…

The following year was when Gemma would leave. That was a bad time, as I loved her very much, as Lauryn also did. Maybe things would have worked out differently if we hadn't lost the baby, who knows? But looking back on things, I find it pretty amazing and unbelievable how Gemma put up with me for five months, let alone five years, as for the first few years we were together I was so completely wrapped up in my fight for Lauryn and was in and out of courts every other month, etc. That can't have been much fun for her, but she stuck by me for all those years and helped me so much in getting through it all with her love, understanding and support. She'll always have a special place in my heart and I wonder how much differently things may have worked out had I not had all that I did have going on during our first few years together... Again, thanks 'family' law!

In early 2006, my barrister informed me that I had a good chance of suing the police and authorities over their three malicious prosecutions; my second Tower Bridge protest, my London Eye protest and the political bail conditions/harassment cases. There was also various evidence of misfeasance in public office against me concerning them all, too. Apparently I had a 60–70% chance of succeeding in them and that I should be entitled to between £30,000 and £100,000 in compensation.

But over four years into the process, in 2010 they were all suddenly stopped!

Some compensation for what they did would have been nice; I could have really spoiled Lauryn with it and I know that I was due compensation for the things they'd done. It's ironic that they can run numerous cases against me and all the way to the end, when none of them should have even resulted in me being charged in the first place, as my five out of six not guilty verdicts over the two years (2003 and 2004) show. But when there was me with three legitimate cases against 'them' with a 60–70% chance of winning, they're all thrown out, just like that, before the actual trial was even reached!

Once they did this, I knew that it was highly unlikely they'd ever allow my cases to run. I could have fought on and tried to appeal, etc, but the thought of another four-year battle, when the likelihood was that they'd do similar to me again as they had led me to decide that I just couldn't be arsed with playing any more of their games, appeals and court shit. I'd had no court appearances for four years; I had my life pretty much together after the half-decade nightmare and just wanted to carry on as I had been doing the last few years, enjoying my life with Lauryn

David and Lauryn on the London Eye August 2017

and Lois, my partner at the time.

In November 2014, I began my second relationship with a policewoman. I was working as a multidrop courier at the time for TNT Express. One of the places I delivered to was the police station at Hollingbury, Brighton. I made the delivery one day and a quite attractive lady called Susan, signed for it. We were having a joke and a laugh and she seemed really nice and so I asked her for her number the next time I delivered there. I wasn't really expecting to get it, but she gave it to me and this would be the beginning of a relationship that would go on over the next five years... which would eventually reveal more of what I already knew concerning her colleagues and with what her Sussex Police colleagues would again do concerning me!

In September 2018, whilst driving Lauryn to the University of Hertfordshire where she was thinking of going, she first mentioned that she was considering studying 'family' law.

With her saying those two words, after all that had happened, it was as though a switch in my head had been flicked on and everything from those years started flooding back.

I'd planned to concentrate on writing this book once her childhood was over, when she turned 18, which was three months away at the time. But now, I wasn't able to stop thinking about it and towards the end of October I began contacting some ghost writers in regards to help in writing my story. Around the same time, I also mentioned that I was planning to tell this story to a few others I knew.

Considering Lauryn has always been my first thought, I texted Jo something along these lines:

'This is probably the most important text you'll ever receive. I am prepared to blame 90% of all what happened on 'family' law, rather than blaming you and them 50/50 for all that you and they did. Let me know if you'd prefer I do that, or not.'

My reason for making this offer to her was because of the

effect my story would have on Lauryn. Blaming Jo for just 10% rather than half of it was an offer she never deserved, but like I say, Lauryn was always at the forefront of my mind.

Within five minutes of me having sent the text…

Lauryn called me in tears as Jo had forwarded it straight on to her. Jo could have ignored it, replied to it or called me… but no, she sent it to Lauryn, once again showing no thought or consideration as to her feelings or what it would do to her and causing Lauryn more upset and stress that never needed to have occurred. So, that's why this story includes so much of what Jo did, because she threw the offer she never deserved, back in my face, upset my daughter again and because she's never cared about anyone but her sick, sad, evil self.

It had now been over 14 years since I'd last been arrested or even spoken to by any police and that was for the Labour Party Conference bail conditions (harassment) arrest in September 2004.

But they hadn't forgotten that they 'lost' to me regarding the two public nuisance cases and the three harassment cases and they hadn't appreciated all the work I'd caused them when I attempted to sue them between 2006 and 2010 for their abuse of power crimes against me. I've no doubt that what followed over the next two weeks (and pretty much ever since) was their 'revenge best served cold', as cold by now, it very much was.

It was during the morning of the 10th November 2018 when they first had a sort of 'legitimate' reason to speak to me. I'd just bought ten Spider-Man figurines and was giving them out to kids who didn't look as well off or as well dressed as some, after checking with their parents it was OK for me to. Unsurprisingly, every child I gave one to was happy to receive a free gift and was smiling and excited because I'd also donned my Spider-Man mask for the first time in over 14 years.

Happy, smiley kids made me feel great too, but within ten minutes of having given out the first one, two police officers arrived and started giving me grief.

It wasn't until I'd been breathalysed and drug tested, with both results clear, that I was allowed on my way. I wasn't impressed that they'd just wasted half an hour or so of my time whilst doing the tests and waiting for the results to come through.

After what had just happened, I had a feeling that, before long, something not very nice was going to be happening, again. Later that day I had three spiders tattooed on my head as it's who I am, who I became – it relates to my 'mission' and, in a way, it was to let them know I will and can do, as I like. I can give toys away if I like, I will write my story (eventually) and I will wear my mask if I want to. None of them was a crime and I wasn't going to 'legally' be supressed, silenced or bullied by them any more, but illegally treated in many ways, again, I soon now would be!

Two days later on the 12th, I was assaulted in a hotel in Findon, near Worthing, by my brother's stepson, Daniel (he works as a prison officer!) I'd booked a room at the hotel for the night and was about to check in when Daniel, there with his relatives at some family do, manhandled me out of the hotel. When I left I presumed it was a member of the hotel staff who'd ejected me. It wasn't until I called the hotel a couple of hours after the incident that they informed me it wasn't any of their staff that had done it, but then I worked out it was probably Daniel who had.

I hadn't seen him in 14 years prior to this day and he was nothing like the scrawny ten-year-old he had been back then. I reported this assault to the police on 101, so it would be on record, knowing they'd not do anything about it.

Less than 12 hours after reporting that, at 5 am on the 13th November, I was breathalysed and drug tested for a second time in four days, again, with both results being clear. The following is how that one came about.

I had walked past a police car with two police officers sitting in it, which was stationary in the same road where I was parked up in Worthing town centre. I got in my car, drove past them and, as I turned left at the end of the road, I noticed them pulling away. A minute or so later, after having negotiated a couple of roundabouts, they were still coming the same way, likely to be following me, but at a distance.

Then I took a left turn and a right turn and so did they – now I knew for sure their games with me were on again. Out of nowhere there suddenly appeared two more police cars behind me, lights flashing. The adrenaline was going now and after a mini panic with them on my case and having done nothing at all wrong or illegal, yet again, I thought, 'What are they up to this time? Why are they doing their shit to me again?'

As I was about a minute's drive from Paul and Dot's at this point, I decided I'd head to their house. As soon as I turned into their road, with the three police cars right behind me, I sounded my horn continuously all the way up the road as I wanted as many witnesses as possible to see what was going on. I stopped outside their house and, within seconds, they were standing at the door, obviously having heard me coming. One of the police told Paul and Dot that I'd sped off, which was total bullshit – I hadn't sped anywhere. After wasting another half-hour of my time with the tests, the three cars and six officers left. (Surely there are real crimes they should be dealing with and actual criminals they should be going after!)

Later I was told that the reason for them stopping me that morning was because I'd apparently asked someone if they were OK, before telling them that I was Spider-Man. Even if I had said either of those things to someone, which I hadn't, I'm sure people say far worse things to someone without the police suddenly stopping them and not just one, but three cars!

The first car could easily have put their lights on or even pulled out in front of me blocking the road, so I would have had to stop when I'd first pulled away. That would have removed any and all probability of me being panicked when there were suddenly three cars behind me with flashing lights, five minutes later!

But perhaps a pursuit or a high-speed chase would have resulted in a serious charge and which could've also resulted in injury or much worse... These were probably their hopes as to what would happen when one following suddenly became three following and with blue flashing lights!

In the early hours of the following day (14th November), I was assaulted again, but this time in the Royal Albion Hotel in Brighton. On exiting the toilet cubicle (that I shouldn't have officially used as I wasn't a guest), there were six security men there, standing in the toilets. They had a word about me using the hotel toilet 'crime' and then as good as escorted me out of the hotel. Before we'd got outside, one of them gave me what you'd call an accidental bump as we were walking along. When he did, I said that he'd just assaulted me, to which at least three of the other five started chuckling and giggling like school girls. Once they'd seen me off the premises there was verbal abuse to me from them and from me back to them, for a minute or so. I asked if any of them wanted to come for a one-to-one walk with me but none of the Big Six accepted my invite, so I walked away. Five or ten minutes later, the Big Six drove past me, two of them up in each of three cars and with fireworks (some sort of firecrackers) being thrown at me from the first two cars.

Realising the potential danger – six of them and one of me – and me aged 50 with them being younger and fitter, I jumped in a taxi and got out of the area as they drove back around, looking for me. Two police cars happened to arrive in the area just as I was being driven away in the taxi; maybe that was just a coincidence!

I reported the incident to the police a few hours later (again, so it was on record), who would have no doubt known about it long before my call to them and probably within minutes of it happening. Security and police, they're pretty much the same lot – some are mates with each other and would have each other's mobile numbers, as well as the basic security police line they contact each other on when there's an incident. I bet the security were gloating in a call or text to the police about their mini firework display virtually as soon as it had happened, especially considering it involved me.

Annie Toynbee, the police's Professional Standards 'investigator' supposed to be looking into my complaints regarding all the incidents over this fortnight, later stated: 'I understand you called Police on the 101 non-emergency number, to report the matter at about 8 am in the morning, some seven hours after the incident, by which time any opportunity for physical evidence was lost.'

'Lost'... after seven hours! I think you might be a little wrong about this point, 'Investigator' – CCTV lasts a tad longer than seven hours (unless it's purposely lost, tampered with or destroyed) and I reported it within five hours, not seven, not that the two-hour discrepancy there makes any difference – as is usual – any crime to me is fine, whether it's by the police, their associates or anyone else.

There would have been numerous CCTV evidence of this incident that night as it happened in the centre of Brighton. I know if it had been anyone saying that I'd thrown a firework at someone or even looked at someone the wrong way, the police would have immediately trawled through any / all CCTV and that physical evidence would have been found and secured, even if it was reported seven days or seven weeks after an incident!

When I visited and contacted the hotel over the following days, the manager told me that there had been no contact with them from the police. What a surprise to hear, that was(n't)!

The day after that on the 15th November, I was approached

by two police officers in Crawley. They told me that I was under arrest on suspicion of harassing my brother. No doubt this was some sort of counter-allegation in relation to his stepson's assault on me at the hotel on the 12th.

Knowing I hadn't harassed him at all, let alone twice, as is required to be arrested for having harassed someone, I wasn't happy with this arrest, especially on top of all else that had happened of late. After a little resisting they told me I was also under arrest for that!

Back at the police station the stated reason for my arrest and the resisting charges as good as vanished into thin air. Toynbee's 'investigation' into this matter stated, 'Ultimately, there was no further action in relation to the harassment matter and you were not interviewed about that as it was decided there was insufficient evidence to progress with it.'

Arrested when there's not even sufficient evidence for an interview – now, that's a new one that I'd never had or heard of before... is this real, from the law upholders?

This unlawful arrest resulted in me being falsely charged with assaulting a PC Wynn whilst in custody this day. The two police officers who claimed to have witnessed the assault would have had to have been able to see through a wall, a person and a door or around corners to have witnessed anything, which they obviously couldn't. This impossible vision by them, plus the fact there was no injury from the 'assault' that never even occurred, resulted in another failed prosecution of me when this total farce of a 'case' went to trial in 2019.

With the lack of any investigation and the cover-up from Toynbee, I thought I'd do a bit of investigating for myself. I contacted Lee Craig, the managing director of Pagoda. That was the company whose security staff threw the fireworks at me that night. He was quite pleasant at first and appeared to want to do as he should have. He asked me for the date and time things happened, etc, and so I told him all the information he'd asked for. But then, once he had all he'd asked for his manner changed. He denied anything could have occurred on limp reason after limp reason, before referring to the fact they never heard a word from the police about it and he then ignored all subsequent e-mails and calls from me. One thing he said that did actually sound viable was that they only had three staff working that night. The thing is, I know there were six involved as numbers have always been one of my things and I've never had any difficulty counting to six!

So, I thought I'd ring another security company or two, based in Brighton in my investigation, as there appeared to have been three other security staff involved that must have been from another company.

I rang one company called Consec Risk Management, with my good, old trusted recorder picking up every word to be said.

I was speaking with one of their 'men' and trying to get any crumbs of information from them that they knew or may have heard relating to this incident that was well over a year ago by now.

Minutes into our conversation, which generally wasn't that pleasant, with him giving me shit and me giving him the same back (as his colleagues were giggling in the background because of the way he was speaking to me), he told me he'd heard about the 'fireworks being thrown at Spider-Man' story. Also in this conversation, he came out with, "We don't even work for the Royal Albion." But I hadn't mentioned a word about the hotel itself and, not only was he mentioning it in regards to the fireworks incident, he was obviously aware that the incident related to that hotel and was trying to disassociate himself from it. So, over a year later, within five minutes of a phone call, I had located someone who knew or had heard about the quite serious incident that the police did nothing about, except for covering it up, not obtaining any CCTV and then arranging my little break/holiday… that's just coming up!

On the 17th, two days after the late/early fireworks show, whichever way you wish to view it, I was (again) assaulted by a bus driver in East Grinstead. I assaulted him back in a similarly minor way. I'd been a bus driver for the same company for the last two-and-a-half years and had recently resigned after the boss gave me some grief and talked down to me after I explained to him about the giving away 'toys to the kids' incident when the police spoke to me that day.

I asked him a civilised question, but in a raised voice and in an authoritative way, he told me to mind my own business. His being and talking to me like that resulted in me telling him where to stick his job. As I left his office he said something about me being sectioned. It was either I needed sectioning, he'd get me sectioned or he'd have me sectioned. Maybe he's a freemason and, here's another secret… not that nice a society from certain things I've read and who could get that easily arranged!

Later that day, acting drunk and disorderly at worst (I think I was due to let my hair down briefly and have a little laugh after the events of the last week), I'd gotten onto a bus through the fire exit door whilst it was waiting at a red light. I wasn't being violent or hurting anyone, it was hardly the crime of the century and far worse and more serious had been done to me by the police and others on numerous occasions recently.

The bus driver got out of his seat and came towards me, asking me to get off his bus and he gave me a bit of a push. I told him he'd just assaulted me, which was then followed by a sarcastic poke in my chest from him and him telling me he'd just assaulted me again. I knew I had to stay calm and I did, as much as I'd have liked to give the little jerk what he deserved.

I got off the bus and so did he, which, obviously being the bus driver, there was no need for him to.

He was trying to provoke me more by now and was getting a bit too close and in my space, so I pushed him away, thinking that he may be about to do something to me and then I walked away.

An off duty New Scotland Yard police officer allegedly witnessed the incident, but he stated that I threw punches and, thus, there was the standard exaggerated and lying conduct I was so used to from the police. It was just one push as both the bus driver and I stated.

So, now the police wanted to arrest me concerning this incident. There had been nothing from them (surprise, surprise) regarding the much more serious assault on me a couple of days ago and I was also trying to deal with their general harassment and false arrests, imprisonment and charges over the last week.

I told Susan, Paul and Dot that the police were up to no good with me again, harassing me and persecuting me, but none of them believed me.

Who would believe that the police would do so much (in a way, trivial, childish) shit to someone? But it's far from trivial if you're the one on the receiving end of it all.

I'm just an ordinary guy, generally, but when I'm being abused I don't just lay down, take it and let them walk all over me, whether there's one of them or if it's the police force... Not any more.

This was just the bullies against me; the corrupt might of the police and authority. I was trying to deal with all this on my own, but then I decided I needed to get myself a new best friend, another dog to replace my German Shepherd I'd lost the previous year. And so I went and bought myself another German Shepherd, a pup who was just 12 weeks old – Rolo's his name – and everyone adores my boy. He's so good-looking. The day was now the 22nd November and I was meeting up with Lauryn and to show her my new pup.

I parked up at the pub we were due to meet at in Horsham and, within seconds of getting out my car, I was being arrested regarding the bus incident. Apart from Lauryn and I, the only other person who knew where we were meeting was her mum. No prizes for working out how the police knew where I was going to be this evening and the time I was due there!

So, unfortunately, I didn't get to see Lauryn (not for the first time!) and now the pup I'd only had for a few hours had been taken from me too. I wasn't happy about those two things, but didn't resist arrest or anything as I knew that, in a way, for once, there was a legitimate(ish) reason for my arrest because of the bus incident... And off to the police station we went.

I was expecting to be charged and/or released in a few hours at worst on this most minor (common assault) charge, before getting my pup back and speaking with Lauryn.

But there was a very different plan being lined up for me, if it hadn't already been contrived long before my arrest!

At the police station, a few hours passed with me sitting in a cell without an interview or a charge and this remained the same for another few hours. By now I was starting to get pissed off with them for taking the piss with me, yet again. Then it got to 10 hours that I'd been held, then 20 hours and, by now, I was angry, shouting, kicking the cell door and telling them exactly what I thought of them.

It was after hour 23 of me being held that they finally charged me. They also told me I'd be held overnight and would be appearing in court the next day (the 24th), which was more bullshit too.

I continued venting my anger towards them for all this, as well as the other stuff that had been going on via them, of late.

Their next move was to call in the white coat brigade, who they no doubt would have fed similar bullshit to about me – similar to what their New Scotland Yard colleague had said during his witness statement concerning the bus driver incident. And with the doctors being told exactly what they were, as well as now witnessing how I was behaving, my completely contrived sectioning was achieved.

All it would have taken was for one of these clever dicks to notice it was just three weeks until Lauryn's 18th, which, if it wasn't on the screen in front of them, they could easily have found out in a few seconds with the press of a couple of buttons, from Internet coverage of my protests.

And then kicked in their latest... I could imagine them... *Let's try this, forget about the interview – let's piss him right off. From previous dealings, we know he'll be kicking off and going mad within five hours tops, as we've no reason to keep him here for any more than three or four hours at the most and once that happens we'll organise his sectioning. That'll not only majorly piss him off as he'll highly likely miss his daughter's 18th, but it will also put a spanner in the works regarding him writing his story where he will no doubt expose so much else that we've done to him and we'd rather he doesn't get round to that... And with a bit of luck it'll finally get him to totally lose it, push him over the edge and past his breaking point and hopefully that'll be the end of him. How we haven't managed this by now with all the previous shit we've done, I don't know... Doesn't everyone have a breaking point?*

12: *"Various police pressuring me to fuck you over"*

The official police line about my sectioning was that whilst in custody I presented as changeable and manic. I wasn't changeable or manic when arrested or over the hours by which I should have been released by. I was justifiably frustrated, annoyed and pissed off with their shit, yet again (as anyone would be if they had been treated how I was).

There hadn't been one sign of any psychiatric or mental health problems with me since 1994 and even that was dubious to say the least. It was down to one of their previous games to ensure one of their narks got off the hook the day he bust my eye open.

Even during the total nightmares of Lauryn-less years that could have driven a lot of parents mad, the police/authorities stated on numerous occasions that I had no mental health problems (as I never actually have had).

The two recent (harassment) stops where they drug tested me, with both returning clear results, proved I wasn't taking any drugs at this time (I hadn't taken any since 1999) to have made me 'changeable and/or manic'. It was yet again a most blatant and simple abuse of power contrived by the sick police. It was a psychological war game... and it wasn't as if it was the first!

I recently received the SAR (Subject Access Request) I'd sought from Sussex Police regarding all my involvements with them. So much of it has been blacked out (and it's the same with the one I received regarding my involvement with the Met Police concerning my protests), which I've no doubt is to cover up various corrupt shit they've done along the way. As for any information contained within it relating to how this sectioning came about, the only mention of those two days at the police station, stated, 'Now been detained in hospital under s2 Mental Health Act.'

There is no other information as to the 'offence' itself, time of arrest, how, when or why I became changeable/manic, why I wasn't charged until hour 23, etc, but lots of blacked out text above and below the line about me being detained under s2 Mental Health Act!

When I arrived at my sectioning destination, which was down in Hove, Sussex, and about a 20-minute walk from Susan's, I told the staff that I shouldn't be there and that it was all a head fuck game by the police and the authorities. But they wouldn't and couldn't believe me because surely, the law upholders do not do this sort of shit and so I wasn't happy or impressed with being sectioned again when I shouldn't have been. It was also stressful as it was dawning on me that I could possibly be stuck there for Lauryn's 18th. I so much wanted to be with her, for not only was it to be a special milestone birthday, but because I'd missed out on many of her early birthdays, thanks to 'family' law and her 'mother'.

Whilst sectioned I had a couple of run-ins with the staff. They were acting like bullies, not believing what I said and disrespecting me. Of course, they weren't aware of the real story of what it was all about. They really thought I had mental health problems and therefore, in their eyes, I wasn't telling the truth. As mentioned previously, I wasn't putting up with that from anyone, any more. I wasn't at all happy there as you may well imagine and they decided I should be on medication, when I didn't need or require any. If I refused to take it, they just pinned me down and injected me, so it wasn't particularly the nicest place to be.

One day, they put me in a segregation cell after a little disagreement with another patient. I was told I'd be there for

about an hour, but when it got to hour two and then three...
it was time for me to vent some anger and let it out. I had an
overwhelming rage in me from all that I had been subjected to
now, recently and over the years, and started taking it out on the
cell they'd stuck me in.

As I have mentioned earlier, I am generally a placid and
non-violent man, as my records and peaceful protests showed
over the last two decades. But, because of the criminal stuff
(false imprisonment, etc) I was being subjected to, I responded
in this criminal-like, damaging way, as if I was a criminal, just this
day, as I couldn't take so much abuse and do nothing about it. I
had justifiable anger to vent and this was how I got it out of my
system. If I hadn't have taken it all out on that cell it could have
driven me mad and may have broken me – as was the state's
hope and plan. My criminal damage was in a way, a crime, but
was nowhere near as serious a crime as the false imprisonment
against me, or the abuse of power or misfeasance in public
office crimes that had resulted in my being there.

I blocked both the cell cameras with wet toilet paper so
no-one could see what I was doing and put the mattress up
against the door so no-one could see in that way either. Then
I smashed at the toilet door until the hinge mechanism fell off.
I then began to try and smash my way out of the room through
the two toughened Perspex windows, using the metal hinge
mechanism as a battering tool. It was now going round in my
head that the only way I was going to see Lauryn on her birthday
was by escaping and that was what I was attempting to do. I'd
got through the first window and, it was while I was working on
the second, that the police arrived. It wasn't the normal police
turn-out, however. This time there were at least ten of them and
they were all fully kitted out in riot gear with helmets and shields.

I agreed to let them in, after a while. Then it was the
inevitable injection in the arse and then I was out of it for a day
or three.

Amazingly, I did get to see Lauryn on her birthday. She came to see me in the mental health hospital, which was far from ideal. I had managed to get her some really nice jewellery before all this occurred, which she'd collected from my flat on her way to see me, so at least Lauryn got her present for this special milestone birthday.

None of those previous two months were obviously helping with what I was trying to achieve, which was getting this story written. A story that so many 'up the top' would rather never be shown or told.

It was around the 14th January when I was released, after another seven weeks of the authorities' abuse. Lauryn had visited me a few times, as had Paul and Dot, and Susan.

Getting my pup back after spending those seven weeks without him was pretty special. And what a lovely lady the breeder, Lesley, I bought him from was, for looking after him, for however long it would be that I was away for.

I decided to sell my flat in East Grinstead that I'd bought the previous year. I never really did like it that much and decided that when it sold I'd move down to the coast and rent somewhere. By the time I sold the flat it was June and I soon found a room to rent in a bungalow in Saltdean, Brighton. This was after a brief failed attempt at living with Susan. The place in Saltdean seemed perfect, for the first couple of weeks anyway, but then the landlady's true colours came through and the next episode commenced that was not so great!

The landlady was called Laura. She was a lesbian, not that that was any issue, but her alcoholism would soon be and so would her cruelty to her dog. During the first weeks she told me I was, "a nice, honest, decent chap," and that I was earnest, in fact, "a very earnest chap," were her exact words.

But before long and after a visit or two from the police, her initial opinions of me completely changed!

Things came to a head between us when I told her what I

thought about her never taking Elsa (her dog) for a walk, that I often took out with my Rolo to give it a bit of a life, rather than being stuck indoors all day. I told her she shouldn't have a dog if she wasn't going to walk it. Another thing that didn't impress me was that there was hardly ever any water in Elsa's bowl. I said something to her one day that she didn't like and her response was to tell me that she was officially evicting me.

Things between us got worse over the next few days and she said to me one day that the next time I went out I wouldn't be able to get back in. I rang 101 to see where I stood with Laura's threat. They told me she couldn't do that and if she did, to call them back. On relaying what they'd told me to her, she made a false counter-allegation to the police about me. Later that night I was awoken around midnight with two police officers standing in my bedroom. They had a few words and then left.

An hour or so later (this same night, 11th August 2019), I said to Laura "You disgust me and make me sick," to which she replied in a drunken rage, "I'll fucking stab you!" On receiving that threat I called 999, informed the police and was told they were on their way. Twenty minutes later, Laura was sitting on the sofa with an 8" kitchen knife by her side. I called 999 again as my life was in danger and things had now escalated from the original threat.

Again, I was told they were on the way.

The police never did arrive and, to me, that was another example of the police wishing me, at least, to be maimed or ideally, killed. I made another call to the police and told them, yet again, what I thought about them in no uncertain terms, for doing nothing when there was a serious threat against me.

This same night, my final 999 call was to the fire brigade as the police weren't doing their job. I told them that I'd set light to my landlady, my methodology being that surely now the police would have to attend – but they still didn't. The fire brigade guy told me they were on their way. As soon as he told me this, I took Rolo and Elsa out with me, to give Elsa a little bit of a life before she went mad stuck in the bungalow, all day, everyday, and headed out. Poor dog.

Around six hours later, the police called me and asked if I could tell them where Laura's dog was to which I replied, "Can you tell me where the fuck you were last night when she was threatening to stab me?" The response? "Oh, I don't know anything about that"!

That summed it all up; to the police, her dog's whereabouts was more important than my life!

Of course, I gave Laura her dog back and told her I wanted my deposit and rent returned, which was about £1,000 in total. She didn't return my money and so I kept contacting her until she did.

I'd used the website, SpareRoom.com, to find the room I'd rented from Laura and when she contacted them with a load of lies about me and what had apparently happened whilst I'd lived with her, they then banned me from using their site. This wasn't ideal for me and I had difficulty in trying to find anywhere to live for a while, not being able to use their site, as well as having a big dog and not being in employment at the time. We stayed in a few hotels some nights and then I hired a van that I had all my possessions in, as well as Rolo and I sleeping in it for a couple of weeks in and around Lancing and Worthing down on the south coast. Hiring the van was cheaper than staying in hotels. SpareRoom lifted my ban once they had heard my side of the story. Another reason I hired the van, apart from it being more spacious than a car, was because it reduced the chances of the police finding me as they knew my car registration, and to stop them giving me yet more unwarranted grief.

At this current time in my life things weren't great, what with the goings-on with Laura, the police (as usual) and things weren't great with Susan either. To top it all, Lauryn was away abroad on holiday...

But my mission in getting or even being able to get near to writing this story just wasn't happening and was being made near impossible with things that had gone on and with things that were going on. And so, one day, Sunday the 19th August, I decided to have a nice, fun day doing exactly as I wanted to do, making lots of children happy again by giving away some free Spider-Man merchandise. I bought around £800's worth of Spider-Man goodies; colouring books, felt pens, toys, clothes, balloons and full size helium Spider-Man balloons and spent the day giving it all away to kids in Brighton down on the seafront near the pier. *(see overleaf)*

It wasn't a bad thing to do. Some people may think it was a bit of a mad thing to do (I'm certainly not mad; God knows how I haven't been driven mad with what's been going on). It wasn't illegal what I was doing for there were lots of happy kids receiving their free gifts and it made me feel good seeing them. Some may think I was taking the piss against the police, for them to always be taking the piss and far worse with me, but I wasn't – I had better things to do with my time and they couldn't have been further from my mind. The only exception was, when I first set up my display, the police arrived and sat watching me for half an hour, before driving off.

I missed out on so many smiles and laughs and witnessing happiness from my own child between the ages of one to six and now I was enjoying experiencing that with kids around those ages to make up, in a little way, for all the lost time with my daughter.

My display obviously wasn't appreciated by the police – they were now in regular contact with Susan and with their latest abuses of power, harassment, persecution and misfeasance in public office crimes against me – again... as is just coming up!

Laura eventually returned the money she owed me, but at the beginning of September I was arrested on suspicion of harassing her, which was allegedly because I had contacted

Spiderman giveaway day. Brighton, August 2019

her numerous times asking for the money she owed me!

I ask for money she owes me = harassment!

She threatens to stab me = that's fine!

My relationship with Susan was virtually non-existent at this point, but when she called me in tears on the 29th August I went round to visit her. We'd been talking for a minute when she started mentioning the police, so I quickly (and discreetly) pressed the 'record' button on my phone.

This was part of our conversation:

Susan: They wanted me to go to court; I've had about three or four different people, divisions, asking me to say that you were basically making my life hell.

Me: They're trying to get you to say that I was making your life hell?

Susan: Yeah. I went, "I'm not doing it;" I said, "I'm sorry." They want to utilise me...

Me: To fuck me over?

Susan: Yeah.

Me: Right.

Also in our conversation that night, Susan told me the police had asked if I was taking my medication, claiming that they were concerned about me.

Susan, who knew me better than anyone at the time, with us having been together for the last five years, replied, "He's not taken any since January and he didn't need it."

As for the police claiming they were 'concerned' about me – there was conclusive evidence of the total opposite everywhere. And, she was right – I hadn't taken any medication since January, seven months ago, when I was released from their sectioning because I never required it, as Susan stated.

I only took it whilst sectioned, prior to my release as, otherwise, if you don't willingly take it it's given by injection.

Susan said, "...he didn't need it," because she knew that my sectioning (Nov 2018–Jan 2019) should never have happened just as much as I did and that her former colleagues contrived the whole thing. I say 'former colleagues' because after 18 months or so of the five years we were together, she left and wasn't officially police any longer.

Now, I had evidence from both policewomen I'd had relations with, admitting police abuse against me, 24 years apart.

I stayed with Susan that night and the next day (30th August) we went into Brighton. I spoke with a bus driver for a minute whilst he was parked at a bus stop and whilst Susan was in a shop. I'd turned my back on him for just a few seconds and was suddenly sent flying from the bus – as he literally kicked me off it. I landed face first on the pavement, half on top of Rolo who, in a way, broke my landing. That assault would have been clear on the bus' CCTV as it occurred in the entrance of the bus and exactly where one of the cameras points. I reported this assault via 101, for it to be on record.

Two days later on the 1st September, I received a call from the police with them stating they wished to speak with me regarding a couple of matters. I soon learnt that their real plan wasn't just to speak with me, but was to arrest me on suspicion of harassing both Laura and Susan and on suspicion of head-butting Susan. I knew this to be bullshit like everything else they were doing (or not doing) concerning me. I eventually agreed to surrender for arrest on the 20th regarding these 'matters'.

I met with the solicitor I had been provided with, told him what was going on and played him the recorded conversation with Susan from the 29th August. We then headed in for the interview relating to the three allegations by the two women – all were to be covered in the same interview.

They even produced a photo of Susan showing her with a small cut on her nose and some bruising between her eyes.

Not long after the interview concluded, I was informed that both 'matters' relating to Susan were now NFA (no further action).

How weird is that? There's Susan, an ex-police officer, alleging two offences by me and with what appeared to be hard evidence to back up her assault and there was the harassment allegation too. But they're both just dropped straight after my interview… not even a re-interview… It was just – both 'matters' are now all over. But I am to be re-interviewed regarding the harassment of Laura!

It wasn't peculiar at all, really, when you consider how predictable everything else was concerning the police and I. I'd played my recorded conversation with Susan to Martin Tyler, the freelance police station representative/solicitor I'd been provided with, to accompany me in the interview. The only viable or reasonable explanation for both matters relating to Susan being dropped and so soon (particularly when you compare this scenario to other arrests, 'no further actions', and if and when any charges actually took place over that prolonged period), was because Tyler had obviously told the police about the recorded conversation I had and that it exposed what they were up to.

By dropping the Susan charges, what they had done that was clear in the recording and had indeed been an attempt to use Susan, was now far less likely to come to light.

I had told Tyler not to tell the police about my recording and he'd said that he wouldn't.

But he was yet another corrupt one (I seem to attract them all) working against his own client and for the other side!

As for the Laura re-interview, following it, I was released without charge but with bail conditions not to contact her or go to her road, before eventually being charged with harassment of her, four months later in January 2020.

13: Nearly broken, but not quite

A plea hearing was set for the 5th March at Brighton Magistrates' Court for this 'harassment case'.

This is the seventh run against me to date, with not one conviction from the first six!

By now, I was living in Gloucester. My round trip for this latest farce of a hearing was six hours and at a cost of about £80 in fuel. But I had to attend the hearing or would have, no doubt, faced arrest. So I did and I made a big effort for it on top of the journey and travel costs!

Beyond feeling sick to death of all this piss-taking continuing from the police and the authorities, I thought I'd give them back some of their own medicine. The case is a joke, a waste of taxpayers' money, etc, and so I hired a Supergirl outfit from a fancy dress shop to wear at my hearing. I also arranged to have my head face-painted as Spider-Man, in Brighton, a couple of hours before I was due at court.

Head painted and outfit on, I arrived at court to be told by security that I wasn't allowed in!

Time passed with me standing outside in the pouring rain with Rolo and a few mates, who had turned up to support me (for the show). Smiles were on the faces of many walking and driving past; most were laughing and a fair few were taking pictures. I think it was something to do with my appearance!

After an hour or so, the magistrate, Judge Tessa Szagun, overruled the security guys and now I was allowed into the court building for my hearing that I had to attend. If I hadn't attended I would have been in (more) trouble!

The purpose of the dressing up for the hearing was about me taking the piss back for the few minutes I was going to be

Super-Spider-Girl-Man barred from my court hearing!
Brighton, March 2020

present in court to confirm my name and make my plea. I'd had decades of abuse on and off and this was to be my little, non-violent piss-take response back this day.

But even that would be denied to me by the corrupt and discriminatory law courts – as they still didn't let me into my own hearing, which actually took place without me being present.

I had no choice but to take all the piss-taking shit done to me by the authorities, but they couldn't take it back or even risk taking it back just for a few minutes!

Cross-dressers are allowed into court, with many of them wearing make-up…

That was my appearance, basically, a cross-dresser wearing make-up and my being refused into my own hearing because of my attire stank of politics and inequality, which was probably another illegal act done against me this day by not letting me appear at MY hearing.

Szagun stated that she would have given me the benefit of the doubt (in letting me appear) if it was for World Book Day, but that it was not appropriate for me to go in the court to protest, before going on to say that, she "has to make sure the dignity of the court is maintained and I'm not going to have an opportunity to make a mockery of it." Well, it just says it all, really!

One: The issue behind all this is 'family' law, so her World Book Day reference/justification/comparison is as ridiculous as this actual case, just like so many I've been subjected to. My issue is a thousand times more important than her World Book Day quote.

Two: I wasn't at the court to protest, I was there to return the piss-take and there was no real legal or justifiable reason for me not to be allowed into the hearing.

Three: As for her lines about the dignity of the court and making a mockery, she should take a proper look at the facts and evidence surrounding the case that's before her. And on realising how the dignity of the court process is being abused by the abuse of power against me, if she'd ever admit it on becoming aware of it, she'd understand how much of a mockery this whole case is and the actions of the police and the Crown. Maybe then she would seek to have it dismissed immediately and raise concerns as to just how this farce case had ever made it to court.

I spoke to various police in the courthouse this day and not in the nicest, or most friendly manner, which shouldn't shock or surprise anyone. Two weeks later in Southsea, Portsmouth, on the 20th March, came pay back day for me, having spoken to them as I did. I'd been on the beach with Rolo who loves the beach. I made my way back to the car and got in, looked in the mirror before starting to reverse and there they were again. There were six police cars in and around the car park when I got out of my car. I asked what it was all about and was informed it was on suspicion of stalking (harassing) someone, but they didn't know whom. Back at the police station they told me the person I was alleged to have stalked was Susan (again), the ex-policewoman and now ex-girlfriend, who I hadn't seen or spoken to for months!

After a while they told me I was going to be taken to Brighton to be interviewed. I arranged for Lesley (the breeder I got Rolo from) to come down to Portsmouth (from Horsham) to get Rolo and take care of him until I was released. By the time Lesley got all the way down I'd just been told that I wouldn't be going to Sussex after all and so Lesley's 100-mile, two-hour round trip journey was a complete waste of time, effort and money.

I was released without charge after being in custody for a further 10 hours. They seized my phone (to annoy and inconvenience me further), when there was no justifiable reason for them to have done so. And as for the bail conditions, banning me from Brighton and Hove (again!) and me having to sign on three times per week at a police station – great, that's really helpful and of no inconvenience to me at all on this latest non-matter.

It was yet more shit to harass, disrupt and inconvenience my life and me.

And as for using Susan again after what happened last time…

I still have the recording, but they can always get over or around something like that if they wish to… they had before with me and more than once!

But the bail conditions relating to Susan (when there's not even a charge) of being banned from Brighton and Hove compared to being banned from only the road of Laura (who I was eventually charged over), what's that about? Just the usual bullshit surrounding any and all they do involving (or not involving!) me. And when I returned to my car that they had access to for the last 10 hours, my laptop (that was on the passenger seat) never worked again. I'd had it years and it had been working fine… a coincidence that it never worked again? Mm, sure!

Two months later I enquired about the whereabouts of my phone and about the possibility / likelihood of it being returned and was told it was still in Hampshire, despite the 'investigating' force being Sussex. Did they ever actually need to have stolen my phone? There seemed no urgency in doing anything with it by them. It's now been six months, they still have my phone and there's still no news in regards to 'no further action' or them charging me regarding the Susan number two 'case'!

On the 10th May, I received an e-mail from my solicitor, Robert Beighton of Old Bailey Solicitors, Brighton, informing me that the police needed to interview/arrest me following a complaint by my brother. I hadn't seen him, spoken to him or contacted him in over a year!

I agreed to attend an interview at a Swindon police station where I was now living, on May 15th.

Beighton sent another e-mail stating, 'I have already expressed my concerns about the necessity for an interview at all.' He thought and said this and I knew the same, but this was what was relentlessly happening to me, month on month and year-on-year – again.

I was already stressed with the whole thing; the fact that I knew I hadn't harassed my brother was one, but also because in case another assault police charge or even another sectioning was coming my way.

After that followed lots of weird stuff by and from 'my' solicitor and the police on the day of the interview. Each one on their own may not seem that odd, but when you add them all together... it paints a very strange picture!

On the morning of the 15th, Beighton informed me he'd arrange for a solicitor to attend the interview with me, before stating a few hours later, "I cannot expect an agent solicitor to risk their health by attending (re COVID-19)."(!)

The interview was due to start at 6 pm and at 5 pm, Beighton told me he still hadn't received the disclosure evidence from the police yet. At 5.30 pm he called again and told me the CCTV showed me sitting in my car outside my brother's house one day and standing outside his house another day, staring at it. Based on what he told me the CCTV showed and with what I said to him in response to what he told me it showed, he put together a prepared statement for the interview and told me to say 'no comment'. I was shown the CCTV footage during the interview and it showed neither of the things Beighton said it did. The car shown was a similar colour and make as mine outside the house, which was all that could be seen as it was dark. The part where he said I was 'outside staring at the house' was, in fact, me facing the house for a few seconds while Rolo was having a sniff around (like dogs do) on the pavement, at the edge of his driveway. Beighton also wrote in the statement that I had to go down my brother's road to get to where I was going, which I didn't have to do and hadn't said as such either. The only reason I was near my brother's house on the days in question, was because I was visiting my late mum's grave, which is a five-minute walk from his house. And I am allowed to drive my car or walk my dog down any road – like anyone else can!

Beighton, by now, had as good as entrapped me after having me admit to being outside his house twice, which WAS NOT what the CCTV showed.

When I agreed to surrender for the interview there was no case against me, which is why it was just an interview and not an arrest. After all this by my solicitor, there actually was a case against me now, at least much more of one than there had been previously.

He stated that he hoped to join me in the interview via video link.

His 'hope' failed when the video link apparently wouldn't work (which was very unusual with the crime investigator saying the video link normally always works).

The sound was OK as I heard Beighton speaking with the investigator on the video link about there being no picture, which I couldn't actually see whether there was one or not as the laptop was turned right away from me.

As for the local crime investigator, that was female rather than male – fair enough… that was a 50/50 chance.

But how many different female names are there? Hundreds. And the name of the young investigator doing the interview, and who was not much older than my daughter? It was Lauren!

Lauren, then addressing my solicitor, not as Mr Beighton, or even Robert or Rob, but as Ro'ob, like the name had two syllables, rather like you would speak to a friend or someone you knew well, seemed totally abnormal and unprofessional, considering the situation in just how friendly they were speaking with each other y was feeling less comfortable about everything going on, by the second! Him on first-name terms with the police he was over a hundred miles from and had never met!

He has regular dealings with police every day; his office is less than a 30-second walk from where Sussex Police are based and some are probably his mates who he has a joke and the odd drink with. It wouldn't take much for him in shafting me rather than them... as I'd experienced from 'my own' numerous solicitors, previously. So much and too much corruption everywhere.

The next day I called Beighton who denied he'd said the things to me that he had regarding the CCTV. I told him I'd recorded our conversation when he'd said them, that I'd listened to it back and that he did say them. He wasn't impressed when I told him I'd recorded our conversation; he told me I didn't have his permission to and said if I recorded any more of our conversations he wouldn't (mis)represent me any longer.

The way I look at it is: if I have to record whoever to get evidence of their wrongdoing to me, then I will. What was the big deal that I'd recorded him if he didn't have anything to hide? But, as he'd done what he had and it could have been a problem, he wasn't happy.

'It may take a few weeks, possibly months, before a decision is taken,' Beighton wrote in his e-mail before I had informed him that I'd recorded that conversation between us.

But just six days later, the police inform me that the 'matter' is now NFA 'no further action' and that it's all over with (to make sure my recording wouldn't cause a problem for 'them and/or him', no doubt!)

Normally (unless they're informed that I have recorded

evidence exposing what they're up to), the police always take months, leaving me to stew as long as possible before notifying me of any decisions!

One, two or three strange ones... OK, maybe, but there were ten here and they were not only a little strange, surrounding this total farce of a complaint that Beighton had originally stated 'wasn't even a case worthy of an interview'!

And again this 'case' involved my 'brother' who I was arrested for allegedly having harassed previously, prior to it then being 'decided' there was insufficient evidence to even interview me, before my being charged with assaulting police whilst in custody that day (that never occurred) and which I was cleared of having done.

Not long after this 'case' became 'no further action', things caught up with me in regards to the stress and pressure of everything.

I'd spent thousands on Steve Eggleston, a ghost writer who had said everything I wanted to hear when I first contacted him, only for him to do nothing of the sort over the next 8 months. I was doing four- and six-hour round trips each of the 20-odd times I went to see him down in Shepton Mallet, Somerset. He was asking for the next milestone £2,000 payment, after I'd already told him that what he'd done was nothing like he'd promised and was nowhere near what was required.

What a waste of time, effort and money that was. So, over a year into trying to get my story written, I was no further forward with it and thousands of pounds down. After this happened with the 'writer' from Shepton Mallet, and similar but less costly experiences with four other 'writers' who were also unable to write as they'd promised they could. As difficult as it would be and with me being no writer whatsoever, I knew the only way it could be done in the way it needed and required to be done was to do it all myself.

Then my landlord told me I'd have to find somewhere else to live, due to personal problems he was having that were beyond his control and so there was more pressure – as it's not easy finding somewhere to live with a big dog – they pooh-pooh, moult, bark and everything.

And around this time my relationship with Lauryn was at an all-time low following my numerous arrests and sectioning over the last 18 months. She'd messaged me about all the stress and worry I'd caused her over the last year-and-a-half. I tried explaining as best I could that I'd done no wrong (as you'll hopefully have realised by now from my story), but Lauryn couldn't understand or imagine that it was all only the authorities who were doing all the wrong to me. How could she?

I have tried explaining what had been going on to other people, with most of them not believing me. But the facts and evidence don't lie... they back and confirm everything and any half compos mentis human being could easily work out what's gone on with the evidence of everything I have.

However, with the latest negative happenings in my life such as the acts from the police relating to my 'brother', what 'my' solicitor had done, the time and money waster of a ghost writer from Somerset, having to find somewhere else to live (again) and with how things were with Lauryn all going on at the same time, I suddenly hit a deep depression, a feeling I hadn't experienced since the early 2000s. Down and depressed and hardly able to speak, I called Bev. She's a similar age to me; she's what you'd call a lovely, decent human being, with a heart, and she'd do anything for anyone once she realises they're of a similar ilk to her. I met her while walking Rolo in a park (she had two dogs at the time) when I was living in Gloucester. We got talking and just clicked from a very early stage – just as in two decent human beings both aware of the 'shit that can go on and does go on'. Within days, after telling her and showing her some of my story/stuff, she told me that if ever I'm stuck that there's always a sofa for me at hers, and I'm welcome anytime. She's just a top class lady who helped me so much, despite hardly knowing me. When I called her this day she knew straight away that I was in a bad way and told me to get myself up to hers and quick – and away from the shit place I'd been in my head the last weeks. So, my boy and I headed up to Bev's. I stayed with her for a few days and her words of support and encouragement brought me out of my depressed state and back from the brink.

The hardest thing going on out of those negative issues was obviously regarding Lauryn and I. Bev explained to me that, in a way, it was as though Lauryn had been raised in a cult, which I totally understood when she explained. I hadn't thought about it that way before. Think about it… Lauryn had been with Jo pretty much 99% of her life and had been constantly brainwashed against me for much of that time. Although Lauryn and I had enjoyed our 12 happy years together from 2006, all that she had been told from her formative years was still in the back of her mind. Now, add in to that all my arrests and the sectioning over these 18 months and it's easy to understand how Lauryn was believing that I actually was the naughty daddy/monster (as her 'mother' had always said), always in trouble with the police and arrested over and over again, or even mad (with being sectioned).

Something else that really hurts is the fact that Lauryn doesn't actually know me now or who I really am, but that's no fault of hers or mine. Her being so close to the parent who's done so much damage to her, and us being nowhere near that close hurts too. The bond we had which is clear in her first birthday video and the bond we had again when we got each other back and through to November 2018, has, again, been further broken because of what the police and the authorities have done to me since then, because of who I am and what I'm doing – in putting my story together.

To summarise, I've been subjected to at least 20 arrests/charges/trials between 2002 and 2020, with 11 of them occurring since November 2018 and with just two for minor public order offences, resulting in convictions. That's around a 90% non-conviction rate, when the average conviction rate from charges and trials is around 80%.

How strange that my stats over the last 18 years, are the complete opposite to the normal conviction rate, of around 10%!

As I'm writing, I'm now 'up' on the eighth 'harassment' allegation charge since the first 'involving' Jo, in 2003, and without one conviction on any of the six that have run their course, to date. That's a possible 100% non-conviction rate and at least a 75% one – with one still awaiting a 'decision' if I'm to be charged or not and the other at trial stage. On top of those, there are numerous other crimes against me – from various assaults, including with fireworks, to my being threatened with being stabbed over the last two years – all with the police doing nothing about any of them. There are also the numerous false arrests, charges and imprisonments, etc. If that's not harassment, misfeasance in public office, persecution or abuse of power, I'd like to know what is!

It's most blatant and not subtle in any way, shape or form.

The following is my telephone conversation with suicide plot conspirator and crime editor, Mike Sullivan of The Sun, in 2020, in my attempt to find out who got the story to him, and to print it the day before it was officially run/printed:

MS: Hi, Mike Sullivan.

Me: It's your mate, Dave Chick; do you remember me?

MS: Dave... Go on, remind me, Dave...

Me: Spider-Man. Spider-Man, the pervert.

MS: Of course, I do remember now. How are you... you

alright?

Me: Yeah, is there any chance you could let me know who tipped you off about my conviction?

MS: I don't think anyone did, Dave, it was a very long time ago.

Me: I know when it was Mike, but you got it from someone obviously, yeah?

MS: I can't remember, Dave, honestly. I've got no memory of that kind of stuff, honestly, and I've always been straight down the line (press, straight down the line – ha ha!), so… If I could remember, I wouldn't even be able to help you then, would I?

Me: Yeah, but if you could remember, you still aren't going to tell me, are you? Because you aren't going to dob your mate in.

MS: Dave, there's no point in us having this conversation.

Me: Oh, there is Mike, there really is, mate!

MS: OK, pursue it with our lawyers.

Me: Pursue it with your lawyers – yeah, sorted. No problem.

MS: All the best mate, cheers.

Me: Piss off.

And below is my e-mail conversation with The Sun's content specialist, Chris Ball, in September 2020, that proved the article was specially printed in a Sun (that was shown to Ed, for him to relay to me on the 5th), the day before the article was officially published in The Sun on the 6th, adding much more evidence and circumstantial weight to the state's failed suicide plot conspiracy attempt against me:

Hello David, You requested a Sun article about your protest in 2003 which I am happy to attach. There was another the day before which I also attach.

Hi Chris, Thanks for those, but the actual one I'm after is the one with the headline 'Spidermans a pervert' that appeared on 5th November. It was a piece by your crime editor back then, a Mike Sullivan. I'd be most grateful if you could send it through please. Thanks again, and in anticipation of the one I'm specifically requesting. David

Hi David - it's not in the cuttings file, but I will see if I can find a bound volume of the paper with it in. Are you sure of your date?

Hi Chris, yes mate 100%, it was in the day I came down, which was November 5th. Many thanks. David

Hi David - It was actually the 6th - Attached. Thanks Chris

Hi Chris. Why do you say it was the 6th please? I 100% know it was the 5th, as I've already mentioned. I know that because this was the day my protest finished, the day I came down, and I was told about this story being in The Sun literally just before my descent on the 5th. Thanks. David

Hi David. I went to the bound volume for the 5th and it wasn't there. I opened the next day's paper and there it was. I thought it was unlikely they ran 2 separate articles on the same day.

The story was definitely the 5th though, if it's possible can you check the date on the page of the article, and if possible, confirm, and send me a copy of the article with the date showing. Thank you very much. David

Hi David, I am afraid you are wrong, I took the cut from The Sun dated the 6th. Have you considered that you may have seen an early first edition of the next day's paper? It would have gone to print around 8ish and available to buy around 10pm.

Hi Chris, Does the '8ish' you mention in your last message, refer to 8a.m or 8p.m on the 5th? PLEASE can you tell me / explain, how that story in the November 6th edition, could possibly have been seen prior to 14.30 on the day before (the 5th). Many thanks. David

David I have no explanation - I can only tell you that it was *published in The Sun dated the 6th. See attached, with date quite visible. As far as I'm concerned this matter is now closed and I will not be responding to any more emails.*

Thanks for your assistance Chris, you've been very helpful. Regards. Spidey

This failed suicide plot, for my standing up against and exposing 'family' law was less than four months after the alleged suicide/cover-up of Dr David Kelly for him doing similar to the Government concerning the 'illegal' Iraq war, which also resulted in the (democide) deaths of 179 UK armed forces. And the Dr David Kelly death evidence is to be kept secret for 70 years to no doubt ensure his murder stays covered up, following the state-organised corrupt farce of an 'enquiry'!

If, for telling my story I'm to suddenly die, no prizes for guessing how or why! Could be a 'sniper' or a blade, a finale crane 'collapse/topple', some other freak accident or an alleged suicide (murder).

At the time of writing, there is currently a lot going on in the media regarding men's mental health and male suicide, which accounts for three-quarters of all suicides. There are various reasons that lie behind this, but I'd bet that a certain percentage of them are as a result of or from the knock-on effect of what fathers are subjected to by 'family' law... having their children taken, losing their homes and everything of value to them.

Statistics show that around 5,000 men per year are taking their lives. At a conservative guess, I'd say that 10% are men who've had their lives abused in secret by 'family' law in some way... that's 500 deaths per year as a result of how this current system works or, rather, doesn't work. There's no way anything can be proven as there are NO records on anything relating to 'family' law. If there was, anything transparent about this system, by allowing people to see the damage and destruction they're causing and the deaths they're responsible for, there would be a national outcry and this evil system would have been opened up (and changed) years/decades ago, to stop this from being allowed to continue.

As Edmund Burke, the Irish statesman and philosopher said, "The only thing necessary for the triumph of evil is for good men to do nothing." And without any doubt, what 'family' law and the state are doing and making happen – is pure EVIL.

A public enquiry into 'family' law cannot come soon enough.

All Annie Toynbee (the Crime and Misconduct Investigator of the Professional Standards Department for Sussex Police) did in her 'investigations' was cover everything up and deny that any wrongdoing had been done by her colleagues, on every single one of the eight 'incidents' that she was supposedly investigating.

In relation to the SARs that were sent through to me concerning my involvement with the Metropolitan Police and Sussex Police, the following was stated:

'You will see from the enclosed documents that some information has been redacted (indicated by black lines). Most deletions have been made to prevent an unlawful disclosure of third party data (i.e. information which relates to someone other than yourself or information from which another person may be identified) or is Police information.'

As for some information being redacted... over 50% of it is blacked out, including numerous whole pages amongst the 60-odd pages that I received... which, to me, can only be a more blatant covering up of criminal acts done by them to me.

Since being driven out of Sussex again because of what was incessantly happening, I've kept moving home in my attempts to not have them know where I am in order to catch up with me.

In September 2019, when it became obvious I had to get away from Sussex Police, I moved into a caravan in

Minsterworth, Gloucester. Three months later I moved to Royal Wootton Bassett, Swindon for a month. After that I spent a couple of weeks living at Bev's. Then I moved down to Andover, Hampshire, for a month, then to Stratton, Swindon, for three months, then to Gorse Hill, Swindon, for a month and at present I'm in a small village near Northampton with another lovely and decent human being, similar to Bev, called Shelley.

My latest arrest came on November 21st, 2020. Ten minutes after leaving home, I was pulled over and told I'd failed to appear at court in July concerning the landlady 'harassment' (number eight) case. I hadn't been informed of that court hearing prior to it nor had I been contacted about it since, and apparently nor had my solicitor heard anything about it once over those 5 months! Four hours later and after a brief video link court appearance, I was bailed.

I'd contacted the police on numerous occasions regarding my phone being returned to me, which they'd taken in March 2020, as I needed it for the harassment trial that had been set for 16th February, as it contained evidence and I couldn't have a fair trial without it. The trial date arrived, and the unfair trial (regarding the phone evidence) went ahead. It was a triple unfair trial basically, as on top of not having the phone evidence, it was far from impartial Sussex police and my own 'representation' I was also up against… the same lot who'd as good as attempted to entrap me on the matter concerning my brother a few months earlier.

Any harassment (alarm or distress) that I'd caused to Murray, the landlady, wasn't even a tenth of what she'd caused me. I'd left her some voicemails because she refused to answer when I was attempting to arrange to get my possessions that were still at her property, and in regards to a thousand pounds that she owed me. Because of this and her ignorance in refusing to communicate, some of my messages weren't the most pleasant. But with what she'd done I think I had every reason to feel aggrieved about how she was behaving, and by completely ignoring my calls I was getting more frustrated and angry by the day. And this was the woman who'd also falsely imprisoned me, threatened to stab me, and had as good as made me homeless too.

Even the apparent 'key evidence' that the police stated to the CPS in order to get them to charge me surrounding this 'case' is farcical. They claimed I'd left Murray untold threatening and abusive voicemails, and with some of them being over 20 minutes long. There were no threats at all, and 20 minutes was the total time of all of the messages I'd left. None, let alone some, were 20 minutes long! Again the police lies and exaggerations were plain to see.

There was also a major contradiction the other way round. I was charged with harassment without any threats of violence, but Murray had stated I'd left a message threatening her life. I hadn't as there was no voicemail with me threatening her or her life at all. But with her lies and exaggerations, and her also stating she feared for her life and believed I would carry out that threat (which hadn't occurred) it's easy to see how I'm now up to nine of these 'cases' being run against me by the authorities. The 5 years duration of all the harassment 'cases', when they're all added together, will be nearer to 6 years by the time the appeal takes place. And that's another 6 years of stress, and basically harassment against me that I've been subjected to.... and with one conviction at the most, or none, relating to all nine 'cases'!

On the day of the 'trial', I was met by a barrister, Ms. Aphra Bruce-Jones, provided by Beighton, 'my' solicitor. It was very much like deja vu in regards to the first harassment case back in 2003 involving Jo, as in I was with a Brighton-based firm of solicitors, they provided me with a young inexperienced female barrister (who'd done little to no homework on the case, as was plainly obvious), and I was (wrongly) convicted.

I've appealed this conviction (you may not be surprised to hear!)

And then to rub a little more salt into the wound as the police so often like to do, and right on Q... A week after the trial I got an email from a DS Stephanie Bell stating that harassment number nine 'case' has now been closed (dropped). The one involving my ex-partner, and ex-policewoman, Susan Lydon, that they arrested me about in March 2020. When they bailed me with conditions to sign on at a police station 3 times per week, banned me from Brighton and Hove, when my laptop coincidently never worked again, and when they also stole my phone that they had no justifiable reason to do so.

So now I was allowed my phone that I'd been requesting for at least the last 6 months.

What are the chances that 17 months after the Murray 'case' arrest, 11 months into the Lydon 'case', and just a week after the Murray 'trial', that the equally as farcical Lydon 'case' is closed, and after it going on just long enough to deny me a fair trial by not releasing me my phone!

Maybe it's just one of those coincidences, with it all but guaranteeing the latest (miscarriage of justice) conviction.... as a 'fair trial' was once again made impossible. How convenient for them and inconvenient for me.

If you weren't aware of what's gone on between me and the police it would be easy to think I'm paranoid. They'd state similar, or far worse, though with no evidence to back any of it up. Others might think I'm some sort of conspiracy theorist.... we've heard quite a bit about 'them' over the last year... but there's not much that they've been saying which hasn't actually come to fruition and has proven to have been correct.

I'm likely to be sentenced to community service whilst

awaiting my appeal, and like in 2003 when I'd served my curfew and tagging sentence for that wrongful conviction (that I shouldn't have served, and wasn't compensated for), I'll again have served a sentence for which I will/should be acquitted.

The real and only harassment going on is against me - by the police/establishment/State.

I wonder... will it ever end!

I cannot be doing with any more false arrests, charges or abuse from the state... I have no clue as to how they haven't broken me long before with all that they've done. I actually think what they did in 1994 has helped me get through all that's happened since. When you have a load of shit, you either go under or it makes you stronger. Going under, for me, would have meant losing my daughter and that would only ever happen over my dead body, and so I had double the reason to stay strong.

There's a saying, 'Everything happens for a reason', which couldn't be more apt to me, as just mentioned... Perhaps the reason it happened is because it has resulted in me being able to expose it and hopefully put a stop to it happening to countless others... Your sons, grandsons, nephews, etc...

If it hadn't happened to me, this secret evil may have gone on unnoticed and unchecked for many more years or even decades.

Virtually everything that has happened to me since 2002 is because I have stood up against the Establishment in my protests and because of my attempts thus far to expose 'family' law. I have no intention of giving up on any of it until this barbaric system is opened up and the secrecy surrounding it all is removed. And then again, not until the bias, discrimination and inequality issues have been addressed.

Please write a review for my story and share to as many as possible asking them to do the same. The more that hear about and are aware of what is going on, the sooner it will cease.

I want to put some statistics together in order to be able to highlight and expose what 'family' law has done and what they are responsible for. I would like to hear from anyone who knows of any dad who's been broken with mental health issues, or who have taken their life as a result of 'family' laws' abuse, inequality, bias and discrimination being done against them and their children.

Please e-mail their name, their age at the time, the county they're from and the year it occurred, to me at

spiderdadman@yahoo.com

**See, watch and hear more at
unbreakabledad.co.uk**

Britain's Dickensian Legacy-
A history of failing our children

Our government, children services and family justice system have a history of failing our most vulnerable. From Victoria Climbie to Baby Peter Connolly whose father was denied access to him on the basis of false allegations, the Dickensian treatment of children continues unchecked. Child welfare professionals claim to 'act in the child's best interests' despite having kept no records on the outcome for the children they have been responsible for. The result has been an explosion in anti-social behaviour, gang culture and children having children on the streets of our country.

1. The courts claim to act in the 'child's best interests' yet have kept no records on the outcomes for children to support this claim.
2. Britain has the highest rate of young offending Western Europe. (Mori/Youth Justice Board, 2002).
3. The cost of youth offending is £13 billion every year. (Home Office, 2000).
4. Britain jails more children than any other country in Western Europe. 1 in 4 teenagers have a criminal record. (Donnellan, 2004).
5. The UK has the highest rate of teenage pregnancy in the developed world; 4 times higher than the West European average (Allen, Dowling & Rolfe, 1998).
6. In February 2007 the United Nations Children's Fund (UNICEF) produced a report entitled Child poverty in perspective: an overview of child well-being in rich

countries (Innocenti Research Centre, 2007). The report analysed 40 indicators of child well-being in 21 developed countries for the years 2000 to 2003. The Netherlands came top of the league, followed by Sweden, Denmark and Finland. The United Kingdom came bottom.

Denying our right to a family life

Our rights as parents to family life have been repeatedly beached in the UK courts. The role of government should be to protect families. Instead it has been instrumental in breaking them up.

1. Article 16, Universal Declaration of Human Rights. (1) Men and women of full age, without any limitation due to race, nationality or religion, have the right to marry and to found a family. They are entitled to equal rights as to marriage, during marriage and at its dissolution. (2) Marriage shall be entered into only with the free and full consent of the intending spouses. (3) The family is the natural and fundamental group unit of society and is entitled to protection by society and the State.
2. Article 8, European Convention on Human Rights. Right to respect for private and family life. Everyone has the right to respect for his private and family life, his home and his correspondence.
3. "The Children Act 1989 rests on the belief that children are generally best looked after within the family, with both parents playing a full part and without resort to legal proceedings... and seeks to encourage both parents to continue to share in their children's upbringing, even after separation or divorce."

Consultation document, Lord Chancellor's Department, March 1998, p 13, para 42.

Removing of fathers in legislation –
A nation of second class parents

Successive governments have deliberately removed the need for a father legally, emotionally and biologically through legislation. We now have a generation of socially engineered fatherless families. After the death penalty, the removal of children from their parents is the most draconian action the state can take.

1. The 1989 Children Act abolished "The rule of law that a father is the natural guardian of his legitimate child" and replaced the "archaic" concept of guardianship with a loosely defined collection of rights under "parental responsibility". PR was awarded automatically to mothers, but fathers only acquired it dependent on their relationship with the mother.
2. Fathers have no legal right in law to see their children. The Government states that 'it does not believe that a legal presumption to contact would be helpful'.
3. This position was reiterated again in 2001 by the Chairman of the Family Justice Review whose conclusion was that fathers have no rights and should have no rights. Family Justice Review, 2011.
4. Fathers only have a right to apply to a court to see their children after separation.
5. Fathers have been denied a legal presumption to 'shared' or 'equal' parenting which would ensure they had the same rights as mothers.
6. A father's only legal responsibility is to provide financial support for their children, not emotional.
7. In 2008 The Labour Government introduced the Human Fertilisation and Embryology Act which removed

the 'need for a father' and changed it to the need for 'supportive parenting'.

8. There is more legislation protecting animals, than there is protecting fathers.

A Fatherless Britain

The numbers that underline the accumulative effect of anti-father policies by consecutive governments:

1. Britain has the highest proportion of fatherless families (2 million) of any major European country. (Office of National Statistics)
2. 1 in 3 children – nearly 4 million in total – live without their father. (Office of National Statistics)
3. In 2007, 27.6% of children lived with their mother in the UK, while just 2.4% lived only with their father. (OECD Survey, 2007)
4. 50% of children will have seen their parents divorce by the time they are 16 (Benson, 2010).
5. 1 in 3 children will lose contact with their father permanently. (Centre for Social Justice)
6. One child in four doesn't consider his father to be part of his family (Childwise, 2007).
7. 3.8 million are living 'at the mercy of family courts'. (Sir Paul Coleridge, Daily Mail, 14/7/11).
8. 50% of children go through trauma of seeing parents divorce by the age of 16. (Centre for Social Justice)
9. In many parts of the UK, the majority of children are fatherless. In London, Liverpool, Manchester, Birmingham and Leeds, over 50% of children live in fatherless families. (Office of National Statistics)
10. 70% of young offenders come from lone-parent families (Youth Justice Board, 2002).

11. Half of all secondary school pupils have broken the law (Beinart, Anderson, Lee, & Utting, 2002).
12. One in four secondary school pupils now has a criminal record (Donnellan, 2004).
13. Britain has the highest level of self-harming in Europe (McLoughlin, 2006).
14. The UK has the highest proportion of children living in workless households in Europe (G., J., & P., 2005).
15. The teenage pregnancy rate in the UK is the highest in the developed world and 4 times higher than the West European average (Allen, Dowling, & Rolfe, 1998).
16. Half of these pregnancies end in abortion; in 2010 in England and Wales there were 34,633 conceptions amongst girls under the age of 18, of which 49.9% ended in abortion (Office for National Statistics, 2012).
17. The other half results in by far the highest rate of single motherhood in Europe.
18. 93.1% of broken families are headed by a single mother (Office for National Statistics, 2012).
19. 40% of mothers admit to obstructing contact (Department for Social Security, 1998).
20. At Christmas 2012, the 10th most requested gift by children from Father Christmas was "a dad". (Westfield Survey, December 2012)

Britain in breakdown – The economic cost

The cost of mass fatherlessness and the ensuing social consequences are catastrophic for our country socially and economically. Family breakdown drives families into grinding poverty with the worst possible outcomes for our children.

1. The direct cost of family breakdown to the UK economy

has been estimated at £44 billion a year or £1,470 per taxpayer (Relationships Foundation, 2012). This economic black hole is larger than the entire annual defence budget for the UK.

2. In 2004, the Family Justice System cost the taxpayer £435 million.
3. In 2011, the Family Justice System cost the taxpayer £800 million.
4. The cost of state benefits for single parent families is £6 billion. (Dept Work & Pensions)
5. The state child maintenance system including the CSA costs taxpayers around £500 million a year. (CSA)

The family courts in breakdown

An ideologically driven industry has been built around the separation of children from their parents. The family justice system is predicated on maximum conflict and minimum resolution. Courts are for criminals, not families, yet they remain impermeable to reason or change of the system for the benefit of families and most importantly children. The public can have no confidence whatsoever in the operations of secret family courts which are above scrutiny and transparency.

1. Since the introduction of the court order in 1989 the Family Courts have issued well over a million orders for contact. They did this blindfolded as no records have ever been kept on the outcomes for children affected by those orders. Between 75% and 86% of these followed applications from fathers (Hunt & Roberts, 2004), and fathers make up an astonishing 97% of so-called "non-resident parents" (Kielty, 2006).
2. Most contact orders are obstructed to some degree; a study by the Department of Social Security showed that 40% of mothers admit to obstructing contact

(Department for Social Security, 1998). A 2009 study by lawyers Mishcon de Reya revealed that half of parents deliberately spin out proceedings (Mishcon de Reya, 2009).

3. The courts do little to prevent this: contact orders are not monitored for compliance or efficacy, and fewer than 2% of resident parents defaulting on contact orders face any consequence (Hansard, 2006).

4. When contact does not happen the onus is on the applicant to prove to the criminal standard that the other parent is obstructing it, and not on that parent to explain why contact order is not taking place. In 2004 Lord Filkin, Minister for the Family Courts, voiced what thousands thought, "Any court that does not enforce its own orders is a sham".

5. 50% of all Contact Orders are broken and are not enforced. (The Times, 2003)

6. Sir Paul Coleridge said in 2010 that 'if an order is disobeyed, say, three times the residence of the child should normally be transferred to the other parent.'

7. A study found that contact decreases over time and breaks down entirely in over 20% of cases within 5 years (Simpson, McCarthy, & Walker, 1995). This has been confirmed by other studies (Bradshaw, Stimson, Skinner, & Williams, 1999) (Peacey & Hunt, 2008).

8. 200 children a day lose contact with their fathers in the family courts. Because the government keeps no records on the outcomes for children, there are no official figures. In 2010 122,330 children were subject to private law applications – that's 2,352.5 per week. Estimates for how many children lose a parent range from 18% in two years up to 60% overall (Dame Elizabeth Butler-Sloss, 2003). That's between 423 and 1411.5 per week, or between 85 and 282 per day. The

figure is much higher than 200 children but there's no empirical evidence on which to make a claim.

9. 40% of children will lose contact with their fathers within 2 years (Bradshaw & Millar, 1991) to 60% overall (Butler-Sloss, 2003).

10. 93% of sole residence awards are made to mothers on the basis of gender, and up to 97% of excluded "absent" parents are fathers (Kielty, 2006).

11. The courts claim to act in the 'child's best interests' yet have kept no records on the outcomes for children to support this claim.

12. If, as the courts claim, the rights of the child were paramount, then they would have kept records on the outcomes for the children to understand whether their best interests were being served by the court process.

13. In 2003 a Parliamentary Inquiry said this on the issue of court records, "In the absence of data, the identification of what might be best for any particular child in any particular case is fraught with difficulty".

14. "Every child has thereby become 'the subject of an uncontrolled experiment". Mike Stein, Co-director of the Social Work Research and Development Unit at the University of York.

15. CAFCASS, the court welfare service has been repeatedly condemned in various reports since it was established in 2001 with a brief to safeguard and promote the welfare of children; give advice to the court about any application made to it in such proceedings and make provision for the children to be represented in such proceedings.

16. The haste with which CAFCASS was established was, according to a House of Commons report, "a serious misjudgement"; and breached ministers' obligations under the UN Convention on the Rights of the Child

(House of Commons Committee, 2003).

17. CAFCASS came to be "perceived as the enemy of a quality service to children" (House of Commons Committee, 2003).

18. The 2003 DCA Select Committee report commented that "CAFCASS' failure to establish even a minimum training and professional development strand appears to us to be one of their more serious shortcomings" (Department of Constitutional Affairs Select Committee, 2003c).

19. Barely a single OFSTED report has found the service to be adequate and the organisation has been beset by institutional failings which have caused a huge backlog in cases and unacceptable delays to private law cases.

20. Family Court Advisors habitually express views beyond their professional expertise; they ignore CAFCASS guidelines on report writing; they do not differentiate between evidence and opinion; reports are poorly written, badly spelt and ungrammatical, exposing a lack of basic education amongst FCAs.

21. In 2010, NAPO the union representing many CAFCASS officers produced a press release followed by a parliamentary briefing paper claiming that CAFCASS was in meltdown, and pointing out that the head office budget had increased threefold while delays lengthened and staff morale collapsed (NAPO, 2010).

22. In September 2012 the House of Commons Public Accounts Committee launched an enquiry into CAFCASS; in November it reported; dramatically it proclaimed CAFCASS to be "not fit for purpose".

23. Fathers4Justice engaged in dialogue with CAFCASS, but CAFCASS never identified the research it cited and never delivered on its commitments.

24. On 13th March 2012, a Channel 4 News investigation

found that 1 in 5 'expert' court witnesses had no qualifications in their field. 65% of reports were rated poor or very poor. 90% of the experts were not in current practice.

25. In 2004, the Family Justice System cost £435, in 2011 it cost £800 million.
26. In 2013, many parents will be left without legal representation after government cutbacks to legal aid.

The Stalinesque secrecy of the family courts

Closed courts mean that there is no independent audit of family court activities; no appraisal of judges, no assessment of the judgements made, of court process, of delays, or of the involvement of CAFCASS. As no records are kept, no evaluation can be made. Without evaluation what are judgments based on? No assessment is ever made of the effect of family court intervention on a child or his family. Secrecy is often excused on the grounds that children will be psychologically traumatised by media exposure, there is not a shred of empirical evidence to support this; it is based on supposition and is in Mr Justice Munby's words, "in significant measure speculative" (Norfolk County Council v Nicola Webster and 5 Others, 2006). The suffocating secrecy of the family courts prevents transparency and scrutiny of the system and threatens parents with prison if they go public about miscarriages of justice.

1. Secret hearings are conducted "in camera", or "in chambers"; they are private, and open only to the parties and their legal representatives and to CAFCASS.
2. Publication of details of proceedings is made criminal contempt by the Administration of Justice Act 1960.
3. Section 97 of the Children Act 1989 prohibits publication

of any material likely to identify a child involved in proceedings. This legislation makes identification a criminal offence rather than merely contempt.

4. The default position of the courts is that children remain anonymous unless it can be shown to be in their interest for anonymity to be lifted.

5. Closed courts protect adults' prejudices, ineptitude and dishonesty and the system itself. Secrecy, excused on the grounds that it protects privacy, is the cloak beneath which privacy may be invaded without restraint.

6. On the issue of allowing the media to attend proceedings as of right, the media were 100% in favour and the public 72% in favour; the legal profession and judiciary were respectively 78% and 73% opposed. On the issue of allowing others to attend, the media and public were 100% and 92% in favour and the judiciary 61% opposed. (Government Consultation, 2006).

7. In April 2010 the Lords passed Part 2 of the Children, Schools and Families Bill which would extend the relaxation of reporting restrictions further, allowing journalists to report more detail and possibly to report some of the documents in cases. The new Coalition Government decided to jettison this part of the Act in 2012.

8. On the vital issue of court openness the Family Justice Review found that "Our own work has not led us to share concerns that arbitrary or ill-founded decisions are taken" (Family Justice Review Panel, 2011b). They concluded, "we have not taken evidence on the controversial issue of public access and none of our recommendations affects, or needs to affect the openness or otherwise of the family courts".

The case for a minister for men and boys being failed and abused by the state

Our men are dying. Beneath the cosmetic veneer of lad culture, football and TV shows like *Love Island*, masculinity is diseased and in crisis.

History, biology and feminism have conditioned us to believe in the myth of male power when, paradoxically, the opposite is often true. Men's relationships, jobs and identities are being blown apart by new social dynamics, yet there is little or no support for them.

If you are a male and under the age of 45, the thing most likely to kill you, is you.

The biggest killer of men under 45 is suicide and 12 men take their own lives every day.

Separated dads are three times more like to die than mothers and have no rights to see their children. Many are left struggling for access in cruel and secretive family courts. According to the Samaritans, men's separation from their children is a significant factor in men's suicides.

Many will suffer from mental health problems, depression, alcoholism or worse. Eighty-four per cent of the hidden homeless are men. Men are also more likely to die from cancer than women. Every one of these men is somebody's son, somebody's brother and somebody's father, but too many are left to face these challenges with little or no support. There must be a cultural change in the way we treat men and boys.

Many men feel they have been abandoned by society and are too ashamed to ask for help out of embarrassment, or because of social stigmas and religious taboos. This crisis does not discriminate: dads from all faiths and cultures are affected by the suicide epidemic and cancer of fatherlessness.

Worse still, men have been demonised and stigmatised as deadbeats and predators in a toxic narrative that further alienates and marginalises them. This dangerous stereotyping threatens to leave a harmful imprint in the minds of vulnerable young men and boys about who they are and how they are valued and treated by society.

If this is a man's world, for many men, it's a world of extreme difficulty and pain.

We have witnessed the institutional discrimination of men by the state, justice system, local authorities and other public bodies and organisations. This has been compounded by funding inequalities, which have resulted in eight times as much money being spent on specific female health issues compared to male ones.

Men don't tick conventional minority boxes, but they are still deserving of equal treatment and support. Institutional anti-male, 'fatherphobic' discrimination is putting countless men at risk of emotional harm and suicide.

There is an unprecedented public health emergency affecting men. Unlike women, who are represented by the Minister for Women and Equalities, men and boys have no political representation on these issues.

We need the creation of a new government post, a Minister for Men and Boys, to co-ordinate a response to this crisis and give men an equal voice in government on these issues and help break the wall of silence.

But for many, the men's health crisis and mass fatherlessness remains a political and social taboo. Some claim that because most elected representatives are men, the issues are already being addressed. But just because many politicians are men, it does not mean they are addressing men's health issues.

In fact, the opposite is true. Male politicians, like men in society, are uncomfortable discussing men's health, as evidenced by the failure of male politicians to address the crisis.

Worst still, men are now facing a catalogue of other health and economic challenges including a fertility crisis as sperm counts and testosterone levels collapse, an explosion in steroid use amongst young men and the hollowing out of men's jobs as they are replaced by automation and informal, unstable, working contracts that depress wages and living standards. The poorest men are also the most vulnerable. An unskilled man can expect to live 11 years less than a professional woman and the excess of premature male deaths is the equivalent of a jumbo jet full of men crashing every week.

It is imperative that the government acts urgently and responsibly to tackle these issues. We need mothers, grandmothers, sisters and aunts to speak out and support their men and help them feel safe, respected, valued and heard.

Looking after the health and wellbeing of men and boys is not only in the national interest, but also in the best interest of our children, our families and our country.

The victims of gender discrimination and the men's health crisis

The Son/Suicide – Distressed dad, Michael Asher, took his life at Beachy Head in April 2017 after his ex-wife abducted their children, then denied him access to them. Michael's heart-broken mother, Wendy, collapsed when police arrived at their home to tell her of the tragic news. She said her son was unable to cope with the grief of losing his children who meant everything to him and that one mother had destroyed five lives and that there were no public services to support her son at a time of crisis.

The Brother/Domestic Violence and Alcoholism – A victim of years of abuse, violence and controlling behaviour by his partner, David Williams felt unable to leave his home. Ashamed and embarrassed, for years he kept the abuse secret. When he finally gained the courage to leave, he battled to get any help, support or emergency accommodation. His brother said David had been abandoned by the state and later suffered from depression and alcohol dependency.

The Daughter/Murder and Sexual Abuse – Jackie Dodd was left without a dad and emotionally scarred for life after her dad, Brian, was stabbed to death by his wife's lover in a crowded court as he was battling to gain access to her and her siblings. Jackie said the horrific loss of her loving dad left a hole in her heart. On his release, the stepdad was allowed to return home and live with them. Another stepfather later sexually abused Jackie. She says children are abused and neglected by a 'fatherphobic' system and she is sickened that her dad died fighting to see his children while complete strangers had unrestricted access.

The Father/Fatherlessness – Like many children, Richard Castle's daughter was abducted by her mother. Despite obtaining orders for contact, these were never enforced by the court. To date, train driver, Richard, has paid £80,000 in child support for a child he hasn't seen in over a decade. Richard, who later battled life-threatening leukaemia, said losing his daughter was like a 'living bereavement'. He said the state had failed him and his daughter, left him suicidal and treated him like a sperm bank and cash point.

The Uncle/Prostate Cancer – Paul Robinson discovered he had advanced prostate cancer in 2013 when he was 53. Paul believes there should be better treatment for men and mandatory prostate cancer testing for men. He says that if he had been tested when he was 50, the cancer could have been treated and prevented from spreading. He says men and cancer don't get the same attention as women and cancer, even though more men die from it. Paul says that when it comes to health, men are being left behind – men's health is dramatically underfunded.

The Grandfather/Contact Denial – Heart-broken granddad, Stuart Thompson, battled for years in the family courts to see his granddaughters before succumbing to cancer, without ever seeing them again. His wife, Alison, said grandparents have no rights and that their treatment was unbelievably cruel. Worst still, she said, the children never got to know what a great granddad he was.

The facts about the men's health crisis – the cancer of fatherlessness

1. More than 1 in 3 children never see their father again after their parents separate. Mishcon de Reya, 2009.
2. Over 3 million children live in fatherless homes. Office for National Statistics, Labour Force Survey, 2010.
3. 1 in 4 children do not consider their father to be part of their family. Childwise, 2007.
4. More boys aged 15 have a smartphone than live with their father. Centre for Social Justice, 2014.
5. Fatherless young people are almost 70 per cent more likely to take drugs and 76 per cent more likely to get involved in crime. Addaction, 2011.
6. The cost of family breakdown across the UK is £48bn a year. Relationships Foundation, 2016.
7. Almost 50% of men who take a paternity test turn out not to be the real father. BioClinics DNA Clinic.

The male suicide epidemic

1. Suicide is the biggest killer of men under 45 in the UK. CALM, 2015.
2. Twelve men take their own lives every day. CALM, 2015.
3. Dads are 3 x more likely to die after separation than

mothers. Department for Work & Pensions, 2015.

4. Separation from children appears to be a significant factor in some men's suicides. Men, Suicide And Society, The Samaritans, 2012.

5. Divorced men are three times more likely to take their own lives. The Samaritans, 2015.

6. Over 100 dads are believed to have killed themselves because of demands from the Child Support Agency. Daily Mirror, 2006.

7. Because of social stigma and religious taboos, male suicide is significantly underreported, or deaths wrongly attributed to other causes such as 'accidental' or 'undetermined intent' by coroners. Samaritans, Men Suicide and Society Research Report, 2012.

8. Suicide remains an inequity, with men and deprived groups disproportionately affected. Andrew Sim, Executive Director, Samaritans, Scotland.

9. Nearly 4 x more men die from suicide than in road traffic accidents. Parliamentary Health Select Committee, 2016/Department for Transport, 2015.

10. The suicides of dads are not included in any data despite men aged 45–54 being the highest risk group.

The men's health crisis

1. Violence: Men are twice as likely to be victims of violent crime and 40% of domestic violence victims are male. British Crime Survey 2011/12, 2008.
2. Cancer: 53% of all cancer deaths are men − 237 men die from cancer every day. Cancer Research UK, 2014.
3. Homelessness: 84% of the hidden homeless are men. Crisis, 2011.
4. Prison: There has been a 92% rise in the prison population since 1993 of which 95% are men, 81,268 men are now in prison.[1] /
5. Fertility: Sperm counts have fallen by 60% in 40 years risking a fertility crisis. Hebrew University of Jerusalem, 2017.
6. Low Testosterone: Men with a lower level of testosterone have a 33% increased risk of dying[2] and low testosterone is linked to depression, obesity, tiredness and erectile dysfunction.[3]
7. Steroids: Steroid use amongst men has quadrupled in one year. Office for National Statistics, 2017.
8. Employment: The number of men in low-paid and part-time work has increased 400% in the past 20 years[4]* and men who work part part-time now earn less than part-time women.[5]** *Institute for Fiscal Studies, 2017 **Office for National Statistics, Annual Survey for Hours

1. HM Prison and Probation Service, April 2017
2. University of California, 2011
3. WebMD, 2014
4. Institute for Fiscal Studies, 2017
5. Office for National Statistics, Annual Survey for Hours and Earnings Statistical Bulletin, 2013

and Earnings Statistical Bulletin, 2013.

9. Life Expectancy: An unskilled man can expect to live 11 years less than a professional woman. The Department of Health.

The funding inequalities behind the men's health crisis

1. For every £8 spent on women's health, just £1 is spent on male health. Men's Health Forum, Royal College ofNursing.

2. Eight times as much money is spent on specific female health issues as on male ones. The Department of Health.

3. The excess of premature male deaths is the equivalent of a jumbo jet full of men crashing every week. The Department of Health.

4. Just 1.7% of funding for road safety is spent on suicide prevention, yet men are nearly 4 x more likely to die from suicide than in road traffic accidents. £8.3m spent on Suicide Prevention, Department of Health, 2017 / £470m spent on road safety, Pacts.

Institutional discrimination: the family courts in crisis

1. Every day 200 children are separated from their fathers in the family courts.

2. 97% of non-resident parents are dads who are denied parental equality and shared parenting because of their gender. In effect, 97% of dads are regarded as 'unfit' to share in the parenting of their children. Kielty, S. Journal of Law, Policy and the Family, University of East Anglia, 2006.

3. The government has rejected parental equality for separated dads, rejected shared parenting, and rejected a legal presumption of contact between fathers and their children.

4. "Judges are being brought out of retirement to cope with the 'family' law crisis." The Lord Chief Justice, Lord Thomas of Cwmgiedd, 2017.

5. 50% of all court orders are broken. The Times, 2002.

6. More than 100,000 children were involved in family court cases over the past year. Cafcass, 2017.

7. 3.8 million children are living 'at the mercy of family courts' after their parents separate. Sir Paul Coleridge, Daily Mail, 14/7/11.

8. There is no government support for separated fathers, yet separated mothers have a wealth of publicly funded supported services including support workers, Women's Aid and access to free legal aid.

The solution: help stop men dying

1. A Minister For Men & and Boys: Men and boys urgently need a voice in government and political representation for men's issues, with a Minister focused on co-ordinating a strategy to deal with the men's health crisis.

2. National Safety Net: A fully funded safety net for men and boys including a national Life Line and health strategy targeting the causes of male suicide, depression and other health issues, as well as supporting men in difficulty.

3. Parental Equality: Having a father is a human right. Dads should be treated equally and with dignity by the courts and the state and their right to family life respected. That means automatic parental responsibility for all fathers and a legal presumption of shared parenting and child support.

4. A National Conversation: Let's break the political and social taboo around men's health and fatherlessness and bring men and women together in unity to make a difference to the lives of millions of men and boys.

Children should not always be left with the mum. The 'real' evidence needs to be considered and taken into account, not ignored, and/or overlooked.

When will we learn?

Yesterday, another mum was sent to prison for stabbing her children to death.

That isn't to say fathers don't commit equally heinous crimes, because they do.

But what is desperately frustrating and tragic, is that we keep putting children at risk because of our obsession with demonising dads when they are statistically the safest parent for a child to be with.

A father is, generally, the child's natural protector.

Yet, upon entering our cruel and degrading family justice system, fathers are judged to be an automatic risk to their kids. They are risk-assessed by Cafcass, tortured with the dangled opportunity of pathetic 'contact' with their children, whilst the 'mother' can bring home the next Peter Sutcliffe, Roy Whiting or Ian Huntley and nobody gives a damn.

Our Dickensian legacy of failing to protect children is a national disgrace.

Below is a roll- call of shame; the tragic kids who lost their lives because, in too many cases, mums were judged to be incapable of harming their children and their fathers were denied any access to them – often on the basis of false allegations.

Sigmund Freud was famously quoted as saying, "I cannot think of any need in childhood as strong as the need for a father's protection."

Being unable to protect your child is every dad's worst nightmare. The courts and child protections services must stop gender stereotyping.

For our children's sake, they must accept that abuse has no gender.

BRITAIN'S ROLL- CALL OF SHAME

1. Baby Peter Connolly, aged 17 months: Beaten to death. Father denied access to his son on the basis of false allegations. https://en.wikipedia.org/wiki/Death_of_Baby_P

2. Daniel Pelka, aged 4: Starved to death. Father separated from his son. https://en.wikipedia.org/wiki/Murder_of_Daniel_Pelka

3. Hamzah Khan, aged 4: Starved to death. Father denied access to his son. http://www.bbc.co.uk/news/uk-england-24388175

4. Mikaeel Kular, aged 3: Killed by his mother who then dumped & and hid his body. The father, Zahid Saeed, was denied access to his son, then denied access by Social Services to his daughter, even after the mother had been sent to prison. The mother still had access to their daughter. http://www.mirror.co.uk/news/uk-news/mikaeel-kular-mum-living-luxury-7039163

5. Blake Fowler, aged 7: Killed by his mother and boyfriend after suffering a catalogue of abuse, often arriving at school with bruises and once being admitted to hospital with a swollen penis. The father was separated from the mother. http://www.bbc.com/news/uk-england-hampshire-31514908

6. Ayeeshia Jane Smith, aged 21 months: Suffered 120 injuries from her mum and partner which were likened

to those of a car crash victim. Father separated from his daughter and had raised concerns with social services. Ayeeshia's father, Ricky Booth, said of social services, "When they gave her back to her mum they signed her death warrant. They handed her back to a murderess and her thug boyfriend. I wish they had given me the opportunity. She would have been fed, clothed, loved —— and still alive. But social services thought they knew better." http://www.thesun.co.uk/sol/homepage/news/7064527/Agony-of-Ricky-Booth-at-murder-of-daughter-Ayeeshia.html

7. Liam Fee, aged 2: Murdered by mum and her partner. http://www.thesun.co.uk/sol/homepage/news/7130241/Liam-Fee-murder-trial-Jurors-weep-as-they-see-video-of-lifeless-toddler.html

8. Keegan Downer, aged 18 months: Murdered by foster mum, Kandyce Downer. Sustained over 200 injuries.

9. http://www.thesun.co.uk/sol/homepage/news/7126510/Pictured-Horror-injuries-of-tragic-tot-battered-to-death-by-her-evil-foster-mum.html

10. Evelyn Lupidi, aged 3 and Jasmine Weaver, aged 17 months: Stabbed to death by mum. http://www.thesun.co.uk/sol/homepage/news/7137588/Mum-stabbed-daughters-aged-3-and-17-months-to-death-and-said-if-I-cant-have-them-he-cant-them-either.html

Printed in Great Britain
by Amazon